JB JOSSEY-BASS™
A Wiley Brand

Social Media & Communications Technology

Essential Strategies for Nonprofits and Associations

Scott C. Stevenson, Editor

WILEY

978-1-118-69152-6   ISBN

978-1-118-70394-6   ISBN (online)

Social Media and Communications Technology:

Essential Strategies for Nonprofits and Associations

Published by

Stevenson, Inc.

P.O. Box 4528 • Sioux City, Iowa • 51104

Phone 712.239.3010 • Fax 712.239.2166

www.stevensoninc.com

Social Media and Communications Technology

TABLE OF CONTENTS

Social Media and Communications Technology

TABLE OF CONTENTS

Social Media and Communications Technology

SOCIAL NETWORKING BASICS: FACEBOOK, TWITTER AND LINKEDIN

Whether your organization has jumped into the social media pool with both feet or is just dabbling in the shallows, it's clear that these fast-evolving services are here to stay — and that organizations that can effectively leverage them will hold a decided advantage over organizations that can't. Harness the power of the social media phenomenon with the following ideas and strategies.

Four Points to Consider When Launching Facebook Presence

Like many nonprofits, the Ronald McDonald House Charities of the Capital Region, Inc. (Albany, NY) has a page on Facebook (www.facebook.com).

Why have a Facebook page? "We've found Facebook to be most beneficial in helping us acquire new volunteers, securing wish list items and promoting events," says Jeff Yule, executive director.

Still, Yule acknowledges, it has not been without challenges. He shares advice based on his experience for other organizations seeking to launch or improve their Facebook presence:

- ❏ **Update status frequently.** "Do so especially for events," says Yule. "You really need to put something on about each event several times or it falls off the Facebook radar."

- ❏ **Encourage and foster friend interaction.** Yule says they are likely to get the most response when they are asking questions such as, "What were your best experiences at the house?" or "How can we improve what we do?" He notes that they haven't done more of that because of concerns that no one will respond or that someone will respond negatively.

- ❏ **Don't be too eager to acquire Facebook friends.** In the beginning, Yule says, they acquired friends fairly rapidly, even holding a contest for the person who acquired the most friends for the house. Over time, they realized they didn't want the false bravado of high numbers. They wanted people to be friends because they really cared about the work of the house. So, Yule says, "We're trying to be more judicious in gathering friends."

- ❏ **Discuss how to address difficult or sensitive topics.** Yule says he remembers a day when the child of one of their house families passed away. "That was on the hearts and minds of every one of our staff and volunteers. It wasn't really appropriate to put that on Facebook, but it also wasn't appropriate to put something light-hearted. So we didn't put anything."

Source: Jeff Yule, Executive Director, Ronald McDonald House Charities of the Capital Region, Inc., Albany, NY. Phone (518) 438-2655. E-mail: jyule@rmhcofalbany.org

Tweets Show Twitter's Value

The phenomenon known as Twitter is impossible to ignore. Twitter.com is a social networking and microblogging service that enables its users to send and read messages known as tweets — text-based posts of up to 140 characters — to persons who subscribe to the author's Twitter account.

As of April 2010, Twitter officials reported 105 million registered users, with an estimated 300,000 new users per day.

Still, many professional communicators still grapple with how to measure Twitter's value and justify its use for their cause.

Why should nonprofits Twitter? Because the site can be leveraged as a way to promote a cause, connect with like-minded people and groups, stay informed of current trends and learn about new opportunities and ideas in the nonprofit world. Tweets can include web addresses that link followers to your website to learn more.

Here are eight actual tweets by @nonprofitorgs (a profile that follows only nonprofit organizations on Twitter and has more than 360,000 followers of its own). Tweets that include the @ symbol connect to other Twitter profiles; those that include the # symbol (called a hashtag on Twitter) signify popular keywords or topics that Twitter users search and follow.

1. ATTN Nonprofits: $100,000 Nonprofit Innovation Award from the @DruckerInst

2. By 2030 the world will consume 47 percent more oil than it did in 2003. @RepowerAmerica @1Sky @350 @NRDC @SolarFund

3. 25 percent of US nonprofits could lose tax-exempt status at midnight May 15 - small NPOs are most at risk (Via @rjleaman)

4. With less than 3,200 left in the wild, tigers are on the brink of extinction. @WildlifeRescue @WildAid @wspa || #EarthDay

5. Good example of a nonprofit with a text-to-give pitch on their Twitter background: @CARE_package Know of others?

6. Info about USA Today's #America Wants hashtag campaign for charity

7. #CharityTuesday || Review a nonprofit @GreatNonprofits!

8. 20,000 Nonprofit Organizations on Twitter!

SOCIAL NETWORKING BASICS: FACEBOOK, TWITTER AND LINKEDIN

Facebook Helps Reach Young Alumni

The newest generation of philanthropists is growing up online, interconnected and savvy about the Internet and technology in myriad ways. To stay vital, nonprofits must incorporate these latest technology tools into their communications vehicles.

Officials with Kimball Union Academy (Meriden, NH) did just that in the summer of 2008 by launching a Facebook page (www.facebook.com/pages/Meriden-NH/Kimball-Union-Academy/15251689582?ref=ts).

Julia Brennan, director of communications and one of three staff members who promote and manage the page, says since the launch they have gained 467 fans (10 percent of alumni).

"Although we haven't fully implemented our plan to promote the page, we anticipated the launch of the Facebook page would be a powerful vehicle for connecting with young alumni, and the demographics reflect this," she says.

Through an Insights feature in Facebook, organizations can obtain data about fans' profiles. Fans in the 18-24 and 25-34 age groups have been the largest groups to visit the organization's page at 39 and 27 percent, respectively.

"We chose to launch the Facebook page because we felt we were losing contact with young alums at various junctures in their lives, particularly as they went off to college, and then again when they left college," says Brennan. "This is one prong of a concerted effort to stay in touch with them electronically."

The Facebook page includes features such as school fun facts, a blog-style insider discussion and an RSS link to the organization's website news page.

Source: Julia Brennan, Director of Communications, Kimball Union Academy, Meriden, NH. Phone (603) 469-2332. E-mail: jbrennan@kua.org

---

Considering a Facebook Page?

Wonder if a Facebook page is right for your organization? Here are some advantages of such a Web page compared to a user profile:

✓ Facebook pages are visible to everyone online, even people not logged in to Facebook. A user profile can only be seen by the user's friends and others in their networks.

✓ Facebook pages can have an unlimited number of fans. Regular users can have up to 5,000 friends.

✓ Users can automatically support an organization's Facebook page without confirmation. User profiles must approve incoming friend requests.

✓ Facebook lets you send updates to all your friends. User profiles cannot message all their friends at once.

One downside to a Facebook page is that you will be unable to access your fan's personal contact information.

Seven Tips for Launching Your Nonprofit's Facebook Page

To create a Facebook page while making sure it's a hit with your fans:

1. **Create a free user profile.** Go to facebook.com and click sign up. You'll fill out basic information, receive a confirmation e-mail and click the link in the e-mail. You now have a user profile.

2. **To create a Facebook page, go to www.facebook.com/pages/create.php.** Type the name of the page exactly as you want it to appear and as you think users will search for it. Remember, you won't be able to change the name later.

3. **Select the category of your organization,** for example, a school would select education.

4. **Add content and publish your page.** Choose information that showcases your staff, donors and volunteers. Remember, the stronger the page you create, the more of an effect it has on viewers.

5. **Update your page frequently.** The more often you add new content, the more often people will come back to your page. You can also send updates to your fans to announce news and events.

6. **Harness the power of news feeds.** News feeds on user home pages tell them what their friends are doing. When a user becomes your fan, the news feed feature tells their friends and invites them to become fans, too, which can lead to alumni and friends connecting to your nonprofit.

7. **Choose the application best for you.** While your page comes installed with basic applications, you can build your own applications that are more useful to your constituents.

SOCIAL NETWORKING BASICS: FACEBOOK, TWITTER AND LINKEDIN

LinkedIn Brings Jobs to Members

What do you get when you cross the difficulty of the current job market and LinkedIn (www.linkedin.com)? A great opportunity to reach out to your members with a very useful resource, says Barbara Bessmer Henry, director of alumni relations, Oglethorpe University (Atlanta, GA).

Using this networking tool, university staff assist unemployed or underemployed persons, Henry says. When alumni send information about jobs and internship opportunities, university staff quickly post that information on Oglethorpe's LinkedIn page. People can respond and apply for positions immediately.

Henry says this immediate type of give-and-take is critical in today's super-competitive job market. "There's no time to send out a mailing. By the time you did, the job would be gone. The information has to be quick and in one central location."

Henry says the service is one they are happy to offer. "It's like a little bit of psychological good will we can share."

Source: Barbara Bessmer Henry, Director of Alumni Relations, Oglethorpe University, Atlanta, GA. Phone (404) 364-8443. E-mail: bhenry@Oglethorpe.edu

Maximize Your Message on Twitter in 140 Characters or Less

A nonprofit's Twitter account can be a gold mine for fundraising, volunteer outreach, marketing and publicity. The trick is figuring out how to best communicate your organization's purpose and needs in Twitspeak.

For example, one rule of Twitter is that each tweet can contain no more than 140 characters of type, including punctuation and spaces. So what can you convey in such a short space that can result in a positive change in your organization's bottom line, membership base or press coverage?

Jennifer Roccanti, development associate at Miriam's Kitchen, a Washington, D.C.-based provider of meals and essential services for the homeless, uses Twitter daily.

"We've found that people genuinely want to make a difference in the lives of our guests," says Roccanti, "and Twitter is one way we can connect our supporters to ways they can help." Here are her recommendations for tweeting to your best advantage.

Use recurring headers. Many Miriam's Kitchen tweets begin "One Thing You Can Do Today To Help," and then suggest something inspirational ("Give thanks for the people in your life") or ask for something ("Can you spare a warm hat for a person on the street?"). Other tweets start with "On the Menu This Morning," listing what Miriam's Kitchen will serve guests that day, allowing people to feel connected to

Miriam's Kitchen on a daily basis. But the tweets that generate the most results are those that begin, "On Our Wish List Today." Which is why Roccanti most recommends that you...

Tweet for in-kind donations. More than fundraising, Twitter has proven to be a gold mine for Miriam's Kitchen when in need of specific items. Roccanti might ask for something like, "Men's jeans, especially sizes 34 and 36." "We try to be as specific as possible and mention things that really anyone could do," she says. "We want to give our supporters a quick way to get involved, and they've really responded. In fact, I just got a huge box of books from one of our friends on Twitter."

Get personal. "Our most popular tweets are ones about our guests or the struggles they are facing," says Roccanti. "Statistics about homelessness, stories about our guests or links to articles about the issue at large are usually retweeted." Retweets (when a user forwards your tweets to his or her own followers) are an easy and effective way to expand your potential base of donors and members and to spread your message far and wide — with others doing the work for you.

Jennifer Roccanti, Development Associate, Miriam's Kitchen, Washington, D.C. Phone (202) 452-8926. E-mail: jenn@miriamskitchen.org

Get Members On Board With Facebook Fan Pages

Setting up a Facebook fan page for your membership organization is a great way to unify messages to your membership base. The social networking tool lets you send membership updates, event invitations and other information directly to members' Facebook pages and smartphones.

A Facebook fan page can also direct traffic to your website. Not only can members access this page, all

Facebook users can become fans of your nonprofit's page to get updates about your cause, generating more potential membership interest.

For more information on creating Facebook pages to build a presence, engage an audience and spread your message virally, go to www.facebook.com/FacebookPages.

Add Facebook Cause Page to Your Communications Options

Social networking is here to stay. However, the options can be a bit overwhelming!

One popular venue is Facebook, which offers pages for individuals as well as sites where people can join your group or cause.

All nonprofits should create a cause page on Facebook, advises JoAnn McKenzie, social media instructor, Northeast Community College (Norfolk, NE).

A Facebook cause page allows 501(c)(3) nonprofit organizations to solicit online donations, significantly boosting an organization's fundraising potential and extending an organization's reach as far as the Internet can go. Also, Facebook cause pages typically receive more visits than does an organization's home page.

According to McKenzie, the process to set up a cause page is simple and allows multiple people to serve as page administrators. Before you can begin using the page for online donations, you need to fill out forms to verify your 501(c)(3) nonprofit status.

Once you have created your cause page, she says, have your staff, board members and volunteers sign up as fans or friends of your page and encourage them to spread the word to all their friends, both through Facebook and other means.

Additional benefits of a Facebook cause page? Access to Facebook's group and fan pages and the ability to share educational information, recruit volunteers, advertise special events and publicize news about your cause.

Source: JoAnn McKenzie, Adjunct Faculty, Northeast Community College, Norfolk, NE. Phone (402) 369-0804. E-mail: joann@northest.edu

---

Tips For Creating Facebook Cause Page

When creating a cause page on Facebook for your organization, be sure to control your message, advises JoAnn McKenzie, social media instructor, Northeast Community College (Norfolk, NE).

McKenzie suggests having two to three key people in your organization assigned to monitor the cause page. Page administrators need to make sure the page is continually evolving and engaging your volunteers and donor base, and remove inappropriate or immature comments posted to your site.

Also, be wary of downloading or accessing any applications. According to McKenzie, while a Facebook application may seem like fun, some of them can allow your computer to be the target for spam or spyware.

Tweets Keep Your Stories on the Beat

How are you using social media to generate positive publicity for your cause?

Michael Schwartzberg, media relations manager, Greater Baltimore Medical Center (Baltimore, MD) and former journalist, says Twitter may just be the next big thing for distributing press releases and media advisories.

Start by signing up at www.twitter.com to receive tweets from local reporters to stay abreast of new members of the local media landscape, learn who has left and what beats have changed.

Schwartzberg says he also sends tweets with a URL link to press releases on his organization's website.

Source: Michael Schwartzberg, Media Relations Manager, Greater Baltimore Medical Center, Baltimore, MD. Phone (443) 849-2126. E-mail: mschwartzberg@gbmc.org

---

Twitter 101

Twitter is an instant messenger service that allows users to send brief messages to subscribed recipients using the Internet, mobile texting or similar venues. Twitter messages, called tweets, are limited to 140 characters, allowing for quick updates, reminders, group thank yous or calls to action. Learn more at www.twitter.com.

10 Reasons to Tweet Your Supporters Via Twitter

So everyone is all atwitter about Twitter, but how does the technological communications tool fit with your cause? Go to www.twitter.com to get started, then consider these 10 reasons to send folks a tweet:

1. Tweet "Check us out on Facebook," MySpace, etc. along with the link.
2. Tweet about the achievements of your staff, volunteers, students and donors.
3. Tie relevance of your organization in to national, international and regional stories.
4. Get instant feedback by tweeting a survey question to your followers.
5. Provide real-time event updates (e.g.; bidding on auction starts in 20 minutes).
6. Share links to news stories about your organization.
7. Share statistics about areas of need related to the work you do.
8. Link to sister tweets (e.g., American Cancer Society to Relay for Life, etc.)
9. Tweet live from your own conferences, meetings and seminars.
10. Announce events and issue challenges via calls to action.

Professional Networking Site Links You, Members Online

Could your organization's LinkedIn group be considered a member benefit?

According to Arthur Yann, vice president, public relations, at the Public Relations Society of America (New York, NY) this online networking connection can certainly benefit members and staff alike.

"We know our members have specific preferences for when and where they consume news and other information about our organization. LinkedIn allows us to communicate with a subset of our members in the way they most prefer, so we know our messages are getting through to them," Yann says. "It also gives us a chance to engage them in beneficial two-way conversations that tell us about their satisfaction levels and other attitudes toward our organization, which we can then collect, analyze and act upon."

Yann says the PRSA gets about 500 requests per month to join their LinkedIn group. Not all of those requests are from PRSA members though, which gives the PRSA an opportunity to encourage them to visit www.prsa.org and learn about some of the other benefits of becoming a PRSA member.

Source: Arthur Yann, Vice President, Public Relations, the Public Relations Society of America, New York, NY. Phone (212) 460-1452. E-mail: arthur.yann@prsa.org

Three Unique Benefits of Twitter

Twitter — a free social messaging utility for staying connected in real-time — is just one of the trendy tools nonprofits can use to share their mission.

Mark Armstrong, senior manager, Internet and new media, North Texas Food Bank (Dallas, TX) says Twitter helps them spread their message, supplement fundraising efforts, increase their knowledge base and expand their community of supporters.

He cites additional ways the food bank benefits from the use of Twitter:

✓ **Gathering feedback.** "We have experienced wonderful feedback from Twitter friends while they're on-site at our events, such as Empty Bowls and Taste of the NFL."

✓ **Adding transparency.** He says Twitter gives them a unique window to their constituents. "It's a very close two-way street. They can speak their mind and we can deliver our content in a non-threatening way, making the value of our message stronger."

✓ **Driving website traffic.** Including URLs in tweets drives people to your website.

Source: Mark Armstrong, Senior Manager, Internet and New Media, North Texas Food Bank, Dallas, TX. Phone (214) 330-1396. E-mail: mark@ntfb.org

Create a Facebook Landing Page and Double Your Fans

When you first created your organization's Facebook page, you probably had an initial spike in people who liked your page and signed on as Facebook friends or fans. But now, the novelty is wearing off and your numbers are leveling off. You may have people visiting your page, but they are not becoming fans or clicking the "like" tab.

Solve this problem with a Facebook landing page, says Dan Parsons, CEO of the marketing, public relations and social media agency, Parsons, Inc. (Lincoln, NE).

"Any organization that wants to stand out among the social media clutter should create a Facebook landing page," Parsons advises.

A landing page is a custom site people see when they browse your page for the first time.

Matthew Tommasi, founder of the website The Social Media Guide (Arundel, Queensland, Australia), says landing pages allow nonprofit organizations "to convert new visitors into fans by providing them the information that makes them want to become a fan."

Creating a Facebook landing page "is definitely good for business," says Tommasi, noting nonprofits that have implemented a landing page have seen tremendous growth in their social media communities, some even doubling or tripling their fan base.

Why let newcomers land on a Facebook wall filled with random posts and comments when you could personalize a page specifically for first-time visitors? As Tommasi says, "If you found a book opened up somewhere in the middle you wouldn't really understand what the book is about.... However if it was opened up to the summary page or back cover, it would give the reader a better synopsis of what the book is about."

What should be on your landing page? Parsons says nonprofits should include their mission statement and information on how to donate. Consider it a mini Web page where you can focus on a real call to action for the online community. Once persons become fans, include them in the stream of information and conversation on your Facebook wall.

Tommasi says setting up the landing page is free, fairly straightforward and can be done by someone with a basic understanding of HTML code. Step-by-step instructions can be found on Tommasi's site at http://thesocialmediaguide.com.au/2009/11/01/setup-custom-landing-page-facebook-page/.

Sources: Dan Parsons, CEO, Parsons, Inc., Lincoln, NE. Phone (888) 277-1553. E-mail: dan@parnsonsinc.net. Website: www.parsonsinc.net
Matthew Tommasi, Founder, The Social Media Guide, Arundel, Queensland, Australia. E-mail: matthew@thesocialmediaguide.com.au. Website: www.thesocialmediaguide.com

To Tweet or Not to Tweet

Social networking is fast becoming the norm for communicating with members, staff and volunteers.

Twitter offers a new way to communicate with a number of individuals at once using instant messaging via text messaging or online. Rather than sending multiple individual messages, Twitter lets you contact a number of people by sending only one message, called a tweet.

While Twitter allows you to send a message to many individuals at one time, it also allows you to gain feedback from this same group.

Consider using Twitter within your membership organization to:

✓ Allow staff a window on your day.

✓ Take immediate polls from a group of people — whether that's staff or members — to aid in decision making or implementing new ideas.

✓ Organize instant meetings called "Tweetups."

✓ Send positive messages about your membership to a select group.

✓ Send instant information to members about new benefits or events happening within your organization.

✓ Tell your members or staff what you're thinking and share updates.

Social Media and Communications Technology

ORGANIZATIONAL BLOGS AND ONLINE DIARIES

"Professional" used to be synonymous with "formal" in the workplace, but no longer. Blurring the lines between personal and professional, casual and formal, weblogs and online diaries have given nonprofits a new means of communicating with supporters and stakeholders. Use these important tools to share timely information, solicit feedback, build involvement and sometimes just share a joke or two.

Seven Reasons Your Nonprofit Should Blog

Why blog? Because a blog is a quick, easy and free way to get your message out to like minds, people who need your services, prospective donors and volunteers. And that is just the beginning.

Here are some additional reasons you might want to consider a blog for your organization:

1. **Blogs are of-the-moment.** Is there breaking news that affects your organization? Let people know about it instantly.

2. **Blogs are easy to update.** Unlike websites and other more formal Internet fare, blogs can be changed quickly and easily.

3. **Blogs give a voice to others.** By inviting guest bloggers (e.g., board members, donors, volunteers, etc.) you are sharing the importance of the work you do from many different perspectives.

4. **Blogs add transparency to your work.** The timely topics generally covered in blogs give readers a glimpse of the work your organization does on a daily basis.

5. **Blogs make your organization human.** Overly branded organizations can take the human right out of human services. Blogs can give that human voice back.

6. **Blogs invite feedback you might not get otherwise.** Looking to test a new brochure or see what people really thought about your last event? Invite comments to your blog and you will be amazed at the insights you receive.

7. **Blogs give you an additional online presence** that can drive people to your website.

Highlight Press Releases With a Media Blog

Create a media relations blog to spotlight press releases and include interactive features.

In September 2007, the media relations team at Lourdes College (Sylvania, OH) launched a media relations blog specifically to post press releases. Written by staff, students and alumni, the blog's goal is to communicate the most current Lourdes news to the public, says Heather Hoffman, media coordinator and chief author of the blog.

"Media has become so interactive, that I just don't think the typical press release, all text and no action, packs the same pizzazz that an interactive tool like a blog has," says Hoffman. While they still post press releases in an online newsroom, "I enjoy using the blog to post press releases because it allows others to give feedback and comment on stories. It also offers features that typical attachments do not," such as the ability to embed videos, slideshows and photos.

The college's Web content administrator and the director of college relations, in conjunction with Thread Information Design (Maumee, OH), created the blog center that includes the media relations blog and others related to the college.

Response from staff, students, alumni and the community has been positive, says Hoffman, noting that the local media has noticed the releases listed on the blog as well.

For nonprofits considering a media blog, Hoffman offers this advice: "Be as interactive as possible. Post videos, photos and allow for dialogue. This will give your reporting an added touch where a typical press release falls short. Don't be afraid to make your media a dynamic experience!"

Source: Heather Hoffman, Media Coordinator, Lourdes College, Sylvania, OH. Phone (419) 824-3952.

ORGANIZATIONAL BLOGS AND ONLINE DIARIES

Should Your CEO Have a Blog?

Blogging may often be dismissed as the stuff of teenagers, hobbyists or conspiracy theorists — but a Web log penned by your CEO can instantly heighten membership recruitment, enhance branding, raise awareness about your cause and even boost fundraising.

"Blogging makes for an excellent development tool because you're constantly able to keep your cause, and what your organization is doing about it, in front of people," says Diana Scimone, founder and director of Born To Fly International (Lake Mary, FL) a nonprofit organization that works to stop child sex trafficking.

Scimone says she typically pens at least one blog post a week on her organization's website. "It's also a great platform to update people about what we're doing at Born to Fly to stop trafficking," she notes. "And that's not just people who are already familiar with us, but more likely, people who have never heard of us."

When your organization's cause concerns current events, blogging becomes especially critical, she says, as it allows you to immediately respond to the day's news. "It gives me a place to post information, and positions Born to Fly as a voice and authority on child trafficking."

Your blog can also provide a personal contact for persons trying to reach out online.

When Antonia Namnath, founder and CEO of Weight Loss Surgery Foundation of America (Davis, CA) — which raises funds and awareness about obesity and weight-loss solutions — built her organization's website, she says, "I knew from the beginning that our website needed to be a two-way conversation with the community we wanted to help. The weight-loss community was already communicating via YouTube, Facebook and Twitter, so I knew we had to keep the social-media aspect on our website. It makes for an even closer and tighter online community."

Because a personal touch is so important, defer from having someone ghostwrite a CEO's blog. As Namnath says, "In today's world, it is not a good idea for CEOs to sit in closed-door offices and communicate via underlings. I think it is refreshing, and it makes both myself and the community we are trying to serve feel closer and more connected."

Scimone even blogs her way to big fundraising dollars. "For two years in a row, we've held a one-day Twitterthon (using Twitter.com) to raise funds. On the day of the Twitterthon, the blog is where people go to read the latest; that's where I update our totals hourly. Our traffic on the day of the Twitterthon is the highest all year."

Finally, don't overblog, says Namnath, who tries to post once a week. "People start ignoring those who feel the need to blog their every thought. I refrain from updating about everyday tasks and stick to posting information that has value to the reader."

Sources: Antonia Namnath, Founder and CEO, Weight Loss Surgery Foundation of America, Davis, CA. Phone (415) 256-2597. E-mail: anamnath@wlsfa.org. Website: www.wlsfa.org. Diane Scimone, Founder and Director, Born to Fly International, Lake Mary, FL. Phone: (407) 333-3030. E-mail: diana@born2fly.org. Website: www.born2fly.org

---

Blogging for Bad Writers

Does your CEO swear he or she can't blog or worry that his or her words will sound too wooden? Get the creativity flowing with these tips:

✓ **Go for casual.** "I use slang, bad grammar, bad punctuation, sarcasm, and I break a lot of rules," says Diane Scimone, founder and director of Born To Fly International (Lake Mary, FL) and a former journalist. Writing in a casual style "keeps a heavy subject from becoming even heavier," she says.

✓ **Don't be afraid to be funny.** "I try to make my posts entertaining," says Antonia Namnath, founder and CEO of Weight Loss Surgery Foundation of America (Davis, CA). "I am really a frustrated comedian, so I like to use my blog to make people chuckle a bit as well."

✓ **Keep it short!** It's better to write five short posts than one long one, says Scimone. Chop a longer piece into a series of shorter posts, adding tune-in-tomorrow suspense.

✓ **Stumped for a subject?** Visit www.google.com/trends for the day's most-searched words or phrases. Type a phrase into the search bar appropriate to your mission (e.g., child trafficking or weight-loss surgery) to identify recent spikes in interest.

✓ **Just write.** Write with feeling, says Scimone. "Tell a story, or tell your story…. Portray who you are. If people want to read a news report, they'll go to CNN.com. They want stories about you and the cause you're passionate about. They want to feel that passion."

Seven Ways to Attract Blog Traffic

You post well-written, engaging articles about your organization and its cause. You promote your upcoming fundraiser. You even build a link from your blog to your organization's main giving page, and visa versa.

Don't let these efforts to promote your Web log, or blog, be in vain. Employ these seven steps to boost traffic to your organization's blog.

1. Add your blog to a blog directory such as Nonprofit Blog Exchange, Blogged.com, Blog Catalog or Super Blog Directory.

2. Join Technorati, a blog search engine.

3. Learn how search engines work, and prime your blog for search engine success by using key words and phrases.

4. Make sure your blog is interactive. Offer a RSS feed and allow comments.

5. Be a guest blogger on an established blog. This is a great way to introduce yourself as a blogger and encourage people to visit your blog.

6. Spice up your blog by adding videos and photos.

7. Promote your blog everywhere you can — e-mail signatures, e-newsletters, social networking profiles, business cards, brochures and always-effective word of mouth.

Weblog Builds Foundation for Long-term, Online Network

Three Easy Ways to Keep Up With Your Blog

Jennifer Matrazzo, communications director, Prevent Child Abuse New York-PCANY (Albany, NY), says having a year of blogging for the organization under her belt has increased her effectiveness with the tool. She offers the following tips for making the most out of blogging for a good cause:

1. Do as much in advance as you can. Think ahead and make a schedule of posts.

2. Recruit other voices from your organization to guest author, especially ones with specific insight on topics of regional or national importance.

3. Repurpose newsletter and other content. But don't just copy and paste, Matrazzo warns: "Blogging tends to be more informal than other forms of communication and works best when it elicits interaction."

Online social networking sites continue to provide ways for nonprofits to connect with their supporters and others.

At Prevent Child Abuse New York-PCANY (Albany, NY), for example, Jennifer Matrazzo, communications director, was looking for a way to quickly update and disseminate information. She also wanted a venue for information that does not make it onto the organization's website, because either it is too transient or it does not fit neatly into the site's existing structure.

At the same time, PCANY staff wanted a way to update supporters without the need for supporters to visit the website and were looking to take steps into the Web 2.0 world. This perfect storm of needs led PCANY to start blogging in April 2008.

Since then, the blog has been viewed about 6,100 times, she says, noting that page views generally spike after posts about topics getting a lot of national attention.

Matrazzo says the blog is meeting their needs, although slowly: "We have received very positive feedback. Some of our colleagues follow the blog, and a couple of our board members have requested to be guest authors."

The blog has also connected the organization with another blogger who is a survivor of child abuse, Matrazzo says, "She links to our blog and often reposts our entries on her own blog."

Downsides of a blog are minimal, she says: "It can be difficult to keep up with the updates. Also, the potential for interaction is a double-edged sword. It can invite comments that are not helpful and don't contribute to the larger conversation."

Still, she says she believes that ultimately the interactive nature of a blog will be a plus for the organization and their cause as a whole, "Over time, we hope to connect with more followers, like the survivor mentioned above, and build a strong online network of supporters committed to preventing child abuse."

Source: Jennifer Matrazzo, Communications Director, Prevent Child Abuse New York, Albany, NY. Phone (518) 445-1273. E-mail: jmatrazzo@preventchildabuseny.org

ORGANIZATIONAL BLOGS AND ONLINE DIARIES

Communicate Quickly, Efficiently Through Web Logs

While members would eagerly read the weekly e-newsletter for the Maryland Chamber of Commerce (Annapolis, MD), and chamber officials worked hard to fill it with the latest news, many members wanted more. So chamber officials decided to transition from the editorial model of the newsletter to a more real-time Web log, or blog format.

That was five years ago. Today, that single blog has branched into four separate online Web logs, and chamber members have heartily embraced the role of blogging.

"Blogs are great for associations," says William Burns, the chamber's director of communications. "They naturally build community around a common cause, which is a constant goal of member organizations."

Though chamber officials plan to consolidate several blogs, they will continue to use the online tool to address a range of issues like legislative advocacy, human resources concerns, green and sustainable business, member news and small business tips. This diversity, Burns says, ensures all members find something of interest. He notes that certain topics are noticeably more popular than others, with education-oriented posts among the most heavily viewed. "Things like suggestions for maximizing networking opportunities or pointers on sales and advertising always receive a very enthusiastic response."

Also important is the blog's role in communicating industry-specific news that members often struggle to find elsewhere. "With the blog," Burns says, "we can provide up-to-date information on topics that other media just aren't covering."

Burns cites four key advantages to organizational blogs:

- **Ease of use.** Updating content on a blog is about as easy as it gets, he says, noting that creating and posting an online blog requires far less technical knowledge than preparing a traditional or electronic newsletter.

- **Personality.** "If done right, blogs can develop a persona of their own. This is something we're trying to develop by having multiple staffers post pieces in their own voice."

- **Interaction.** The best blogs also create space for public interaction, says Burns. "They build a powerful community of discussion and action around their content."

- **Informality.** "Blogs are good for translating complex topics into easily digestible portions. In a blog, you can just explain things in normal terms. You don't have to put things the way you would in a press release."

Source: William Burns, Director of Communications, Maryland Chamber of Commerce, Annapolis, MD. Phone (410) 269-0642. E-mail: wburns@mdchamber.org

---

Building a Member-pleasing Blog

To help your blog begin the journey from drab to fab, William Burns, director of communications at the Maryland Chamber of Commerce (Annapolis, MD), recommends:

- ❑ Working to engage members with content. Threads with open-ended questions, online polls and invitations to comment on posts help members become involved and interested.

- ❑ Incorporating multimedia. "Video demonstrates passion for a subject like nothing else," says Burns. "When kept short and informative, media clips are a great compliment to text."

- ❑ Leveraging local expertise. Featuring tips and suggestions from current members provides information from a reputable local source and reinforces member-to-member relationships.

- ❑ Starting simple. For first-time bloggers, Burns says to forget presentation and focus on content. "Go to a free service like Wordpress.com or Blogger.com, and just start talking about what you know. Incorporating the blog into your site can wait until you have built up your following a bit."

ORGANIZATIONAL BLOGS AND ONLINE DIARIES

Student Blogs Can Be a Deciding Factor in College Choices

As technology continues to advance, the ever-changing methods with which people share information require that communications professionals continually adapt.

"The shrinking of traditional media has had an impact on our communication outreach," says Ann Marie Varga, assistant vice president of public relations, Rollins College (Winter Park, FL). "We want to maximize two-way communication and relationship-building opportunities." One way they do so is with R-Journals.

One of the first student blogs in the nation, R-Journals was launched as a pilot program in spring 2005. Latest surveys reveal that 28 percent of incoming students read the blogs, many of whom say it helped them make a decision to attend Rollins. Says Varga, "At an annual cost of $3,000, it is much more affordable than direct mail."

Each year a committee chooses five R-Journalists. "Writing skills are important," Varga says, "but we also strive to choose students from a variety of geographic areas of the country, areas of study and class years. We never censor, but

do edit for grammar and the blogs have to be approved. There has only been one time in five years we have had to ask a student to revise an entry. As ambassadors, candor is allowed, disrespect is unacceptable."

Once chosen, R-Journalists receive training, editorial suggestions and guidelines, a stipend each term and a camera, providing they fulfill their entry requirements.

Varga says the two-way forum has been invaluable to prospective students like Brittany Fornof, who went on to become an R-Journalist and is now a junior. Fornof says the blogs gave her greater perspective into life at Rollins College: "I found myself reading the blogs of a female student attending Rollins. Now Rollins not only had a name, it had a face. It gave me a stepping-stone with which to familiarize myself with this institution."

Source: Ann Marie Varga, Assistant Vice President of Public Relations, Rollins College, Winter Park, FL. Phone (407) 646-2159. E-mail: AVarga@rollins.edu

Offer an Online Diary to Give Members Inside Look

Sharing stories about what's happening at your organization through photos is a great way to keep members connected. Doing so online allows you to bypass any geographic barriers.

One example of this concept in action can be found at www.wlu.edu, the home page of Washington and Lee University (Lexington, VA).

The feature, Scene on Campus, is a slideshow created weekly that contains photos related to the university — sporting events, lectures or just a snapshot that captures the beauty of the campus.

While staff do not currently keep statistics that show how many people visit Scene on Campus online, Jeff Hanna, executive director of communications and public affairs, says the feature does draw attention and generate feedback.

"It's been a very popular feature," Hanna says. "We get feedback all the time from alumni and students that they very much like looking at the photos. It helps bring people back to the time they've spent here."

The slideshows are created with Soundslides (www.

soundslides.com), a software program that combines still images and audio, if desired, into a slick slideshow presentation on the Web.

Web editor Jessica Carter, who produces the weekly feature, says most of the effort actually rests on the university's two photographers.

"It only takes me about two hours a week to caption the photos and load them," Carter says. "It takes them about two to five hours each week to choose which photos they want to share and color correct them."

Some past slideshows have even been dedicated to a single subject, such as the renovation of a historic building on campus, complete with blueprints. The slideshows will also feature photos submitted by students, alumni and others.

"It all keeps people engaged with the university," Carter says.

Source: Jeff Hanna, Executive Director of Communications and Public Affairs; Jessica Carter, Web Editor; Washington and Lee University, Lexington, VA. Phone (540) 458-8459. E-mail: jhanna@wlu.edu

Social Media and Communications Technology: Essential Strategies for Nonprofits and Associations.
Edited by Scott C. Stevenson.
© 2011 Stevenson, Inc. Published 2011 by Stevenson, Inc.

Social Media and Communications Technology

YOUTUBE AND VIDEO DOCUMENTATION

The stories of satisfied constituents — told in their words, from their point of view — are one of the most powerful ways to share an organization's story. The kind of videography needed to share such stories used to be the province of multi-million dollar organizations alone. But digital recording and file sharing technologies have greatly leveled the playing field and enabled almost any nonprofit to maximize its outreach impact.

Create a YouTube Presence for Your Organization

Interested in telling your story without breaking the bank? Consider beefing up your online presence through YouTube (www.youtube.com).

The popular online video-sharing site now boasts a non-profit channel where associations, organizations and nonprofits can increase awareness, promote events and even encourage donations.

One organization putting YouTube to the test is the March of Dimes (White Plains, NY).

In August 2006, the national organization created its YouTube channel (www.youtube.com/user/MarchofDimes). The site now has more than 1,000 subscribers and receives some 16,000 views each week and 65,000 each month.

The channel, similar to a website, holds more than 800 videos, from historical footage to testimonials and inspirational stories to fundraising videos.

"YouTube has enabled us to make use of video that we would have had to stream ourselves in the past," says Patty Goldman, vice president chief marketing officer. "It is a user-friendly way for staff and our volunteers to self-publish stories that convey our mission to the public."

Goldman recommends steps for organizations considering a YouTube presence:

☐ **Visit YouTube (www.youtube.com/nonprofits) for information on creating a channel.** The page includes benefits, requirements and inexpensive tips for making and editing videos.

☐ **Interact with other users on the site.** Goldman says, "YouTube user 'agentchange' is the nonprofit YouTube account manager and offers excellent tips on how nonprofits can rise up the ranks on the site."

☐ **Find your audience.** "Every charity has a target audience," she says. "Search out your target audience on the site and let them know you're active on YouTube."

☐ **Stay up to date.** Goldman says March of Dimes checks its site three times a day for comments, friend invites and new subscribers. Additionally, it updates videos as they become available, keeping the material fresh.

Source: Patty Goldman, Vice President Chief Marketing Officer, March of Dimes, White Plains, NY.

Use YouTube to Bring Your Message Home

Use the virally popular online video hosting site, YouTube, to inspire and educate others about your cause.

When Theresa Petrone, campaign manager-special events, Leukemia & Lymphoma Society (Albany, NY) first saw the video "Jake's Journey" on YouTube, she was so touched by the message that she immediately began sharing it with potential fundraising participants.

The video showed images of one of the honorary patients for the chapter's Man & Woman of the Year campaign before, during and after leukemia treatment.

The reaction was so positive, Petrone asked the mother of the other honorary patient for photos of her child "so I could tell the story of both of these brave children."

Links to the videos appear on the campaign website and fundraising participant recruits also received the link via e-mail. The organization has created its own YouTube channel at: www.youtube.com/user/LeukemiaLymphomaSoc

Petrone offers tips for creating videos about your organization for YouTube:

1. **Assembling videos requires special software.** Seek out someone with the necessary software and technical savvy who is willing to volunteer in exchange for recognition and mention.

2. **Be careful that what you post doesn't violate copyright laws.** Petrone says one of their videos was flagged and subsequently removed because of copyright issues related to the background music they used.

3. **Make videos multi-purpose** to make the investment of your time and effort worthwhile. Petrone says the videos they use will also be used at the campaign's grand finale celebration and may become permanent clips on the organization's website.

Petrone says she plans to continue using YouTube for other society business as a way to quickly, easily and inexpensively — via e-mail link or website posting — send a powerful message to potential donors and volunteers.

Source: Theresa C. Petrone, Campaign Manager-Special Events, Leukemia & Lymphoma Society-Upstate New York and Vermont Chapter, Albany, NY. Phone (518) 438-3583. E-mail: theresa.petrone@lls.org

YouTube Channel Puts University Research Front and Center

How would you like to share your work and get your message out to 500 people a day? That's what a branded YouTube channel is accomplishing for Purdue University (Lafayette, IN), according to Mike Willis, staff member with Purdue's online experience and emerging technologies group, Office of Marketing and Media.

Purdue's public information and media relations staff started using the channel after noticing other research universities — including the University of California, Berkeley — were doing so successfully.

With the help of the public relations office at Berkeley and YouTube staff, Purdue staff created their own presence on the popular video-sharing site.

In most cases, university officials post videos that are produced in conjunction with news releases put out by the university, Willis says. "Other areas of the university provide some material," he says, "but the basic idea is to not put up video that we would be embarrassed to see on the local TV stations."

They include links to the videos in news releases sent to media and published on Purdue's website. A faculty/staff newsletter also lists links to news releases and videos.

Statistics provided through YouTube analytics (which also tell how viewers locate videos and basic demographic information) show Purdue videos are viewed 500 times per day. YouTube also uses Purdue's channel as a good example of a university channel.

Willis suggests making sure you have a plan for providing updates and new material for the channel when utilizing this form of information sharing.

Source: Mike Willis, Online Experience and Emerging Technologies Group, Office of Marketing and Media, Purdue University, West Lafayette, IN. Phone (765) 494-0371. E-mail: jmwillis@purdue.edu

---

Setting Up a Branded YouTube Channel

Thinking about how your organization can get started with YouTube?

The site has a program for nonprofits to create their own branded channels.

The program, for eligible nonprofits in the United States and United Kingdom, provides premium branding capabilities and uploading capacity. It also gives the option to drive fundraising, place a call-to-action overlay on videos and post on the YouTube Video Volunteers' Platform to locate a skilled YouTube user to create your video.

For more information, to get started or learn how to maximize your YouTube channel to benefit your cause, visit www.youtube.com/nonprofits.

Videos Create Lasting Marketing Tool

Producing a quality video of your event is an effective way to advertise the event in the years to come. A video diary of the event posted at your website is also a great way to attract donors and sponsors and feature staff and volunteers in action.

Follow these tips to create a lasting video to post at your nonprofit's website:

✓ Be sure to shoot the planning and setup phases to show the effort put into the event and to show your staff and volunteers in action.

✓ At the event, shoot video of guests and interview board members and specific guests who could speak eloquently about the organization's cause.

✓ Tape the fundraising portions of your event to feature the efforts of donors and sponsors. In the editing phase of compiling the final video, incorporate photos of sponsors and their logos as a way of thanking them for their support.

✓ End the video with information and details about sponsoring, donating to or volunteering at next year's event.

Social Media and Communications Technology

Consider Amateur Video as a Unique Promotional Tool

We live in the age of viral videos — homemade movies and video clips that are uploaded to public internet sites like YouTube and Facebook. Viral videos are a great way to generate water-cooler conversations. Think about it. How many of you have seen the baby dancing to Beyonce's "Single Ladies" and passed on a link to your co-workers?

Lesa McDermott, the co-chair for the 2nd Annual Komen Siouxland Race for the Cure (Sioux City, IA) is tapping into the amateur video trend to drum up enthusiasm and publicity for her event, a charity race, which raises money to fund free mammograms and research to find a breast cancer cure.

McDermott came up with the concept to launch a video contest for Siouxland's inaugural Race for the Cure. "It's a fun way to get a promotional and inspirational video done. When we tell people that the Race for the Cure is different than other runs and walks, it's hard to explain what makes it different. So I really wanted to try and capture that experience on film to show people."

Here is how the free contest worked. People shot their videos on the day of the race, which was in May. They then had until mid-June to submit them to the local affiliate office for consideration. Entries were judged by a race committee. The top three videos that best capture the race day experience were awarded $350. Those videos will be used to promote the 2011 Race for the Cure. "It's a fun way to encourage the film makers in Sioux City to get recognized for their talents and to support a wonderful cause," says McDermott.

McDermott says she was blown away by the quality of the entries, "I still cry every time I watch last year's video." The local affiliate posted the video on their website, Facebook page and YouTube as well.

Currently the videos are submitted by mail, but McDermott says they will be able to upload them directly onto the affiliate's website in the future. The contest went over so well that affiliates across the country are incorporating it into their races.

Source: Lesa McDermott, Komen Siouxland Race for the Cure Co-Chair, Sioux City, IA. Phone (712) 277-1553.
E-mail: lesamcdermott@gmail.com. Website: www.komensiouxland.org

---

Tips for Shooting Amateur Video

Lesa McDermott, the co-chair for the 2nd Annual Komen Siouxland Race for the Cure (Sioux City, IA) says one way to help get better video entries is to post some video shooting and editing tips on your website. Here are some easy suggestions that can make a big difference in the final product.

❑ **Think Wide, Medium and Close** — These are the three shots you want of anything you are shooting. For a charity race, the wide shot would be of the entire group. The medium shot would be of a particular race group or runner. The close shot would be video of hands, feet, T-shirts and ribbons. The wide shot establishes the scene, the medium shot shows what you are featuring and the close shots can be used to transition from one shot to another when editing.

❑ **Hold Still** — Think of your video camera as a still camera. Hold it steady for 10 to 15 seconds for each shot you take. The action of your video should come from your subjects, not camera movements. Panning and zooming the lens will only make your audience uneasy and dilute your video's impact.

❑ **Vary Background Interviews** — If you shoot all of your interviews with people in the same spot, you cannot edit from one interview to the next without it looking like one person disappeared, and the other magically appeared in the same place. It's called a jump cut.

❑ **Know Where the Sun Is** — You always want the sun to be on your interview subject's face. Not only is it a free lighting source, this guarantees you don't have to worry about the sun being behind your interviewee, which could make the person's face dark and the shot unusable.

YOUTUBE AND VIDEO DOCUMENTATION

Leveraging the Power of Documentary Films

Moviemaking magic isn't just for Hollywood. No matter what the size, scope or mission of your nonprofit organization, creating your own documentary can increase your fundraising, outreach and marketing efforts dramatically — with no need to hire a professional camera crew. Here are some real-life success stories from nonprofits nationwide that captured their cause on video:

"Our teenage founder began with nominal resources, but she leveraged the power of an instructional, 46-minute film she wrote to enlist national media support (for this organization that teaches self-defense to girls and women). We grew from a small service project into an organization that has empowered 1.2 million girls to fight back against sexual assault, human trafficking, and abduction across 49 countries."

> — *Maggie Jessup, Executive Director,*
> *Just Yell Fire (Vancouver, WA)*

"Our organization uses short films, which we produce in-house, as part of our fundraising efforts (which help enhance lives of orphaned children in developing countries). Our supporters can get our films free for the asking on DVD. They are targeted for use in group showings at churches, civic organizations, classrooms, etc. We also use the DVDs in media packs and as giveaways at fundraisers and conferences."

> — *Ken Wilson, Media Director,*
> *International Children's Care (Vancouver, WA)*

"I developed a public service announcement about lung cancer to promote a 5K fundraiser (which grossed more than $80,000 for the organization dedicated to lung-cancer awareness and research funding). Afterwards, we made minor edits so it could be used for the cause rather than just a single event. It was very well received during its premiere viewing at the Nasher Museum of Art at Duke University (Durham, NC). So much so, in fact, that it is being used to help teach interns at the Duke University Medical Center about compassion for lung cancer patients. This production cost virtually nothing; I gave a $200 donation to the cameraman and my daughter purchased a video editing program for about $100. While it may not be slick and professional, it gets the message across."

> — *Dusty Donaldson, Founder,*
> *Dusty Joy Foundation (High Point, NC)*

"Documentary film has been an incredibly powerful tool for our organization (which is dedicated to helping children impacted by poverty, violence, illness and natural disasters). I produced a short documentary highlighting the work of our Project Joy initiative in post-Katrina Mississippi. We've shown it at film festivals and have also produced a curriculum and fundraising guide so the film can be used as a tool for teachers, trainees, donors and interested citizens. The footage has been repurposed for mainstream coverage as well — including a spot on 'The Today Show.'"

> — *Aimee Corrigan, Multimedia Producer,*
> *Life is Good Kids Foundation (Boston, MA)*

Creating Effective Podcasts

Creating a series of podcasts on specific topics relevant to your volunteers and constituents is yet another way for your nonprofit to deliver strong service. At Access to Student Assistance Programs in Reach of Everyone (ASPIRE) of Eugene, OR, nearly 10 new podcasts have been created to communicate effectively with constituents. ASPIRE is a mentoring program that offers volunteers the opportunity to mentor high school students regarding their college options.

A podcast is a series of digital media files, in audio or video format, that are released episodically and are downloadable.

ASPIRE's recent podcast titles include "Financial Aid for Former Foster Youth" and "Avoiding Scholarship Scams." Lori Ellis, ASPIRE and outreach supervisor, offers the following tips for creating effective podcasts:

- Create a template which includes a consistent opening and closing that supports your agency's mission.

- Maintain an engaging tone and avoid a dry delivery.

- Use podcasts to provide information about specific topics that a variety of audiences would benefit from or that will help provide training for volunteers.

- Use short timeframes for presenting information. We have found that anywhere from three to seven minutes allows us to present information that is easily absorbed by audiences.

- Create a podcast studio to record your podcasts to limit interruptions.

- Invest in microphones, webcams and software to make the most of the recording experience.

Source: Lori Ellis, ASPIRE and Outreach Supervisor, Access to Student Assistance Programs in Reach of Everyone, Eugene, OR. Phone (800) 452-8807. E-mail: lorianne.m.ellis@state.or.us. Website: www.aspireoregon.org

Social Media and Communications Technology

PULLING IT ALL TOGETHER: SOCIAL MEDIA STRATEGY

The explosion of divergent communications platforms has left many nonprofits reeling. More importantly, the scrambling to keep up with constantly changing technology can divert attention from more critical questions of communication strategy: Why are we using the media services we are? What are we trying to achieve? How are we measuring success? Answering such questions will help you move from merely using social media to mastering and leveraging it.

New Media Tactics Maximize Exposure

How would you like to boost your Facebook fans by 177 percent in one week?

That's what happened with Hoops for Hope L.A., a celebrity basketball fundraiser held in February at Los Angeles' Staples Center. The event was a collaboration between two nonprofits in the greater Los Angeles area: The Arnold C. Yoder Survivors Foundation and Hawks Hoops Sports Foundation.

Facebook fan numbers grew as a result of two online press releases embedded with multimedia components including a YouTube video and a screen capture of the event's Facebook page, and distributed through PRWeb, a company which offers premium search engine optimization and boasts a distribution list of more than 30,000 journalists and bloggers.

"Many people felt that when social media came into play that news releases would be obsolete," says Cheryl Lawson, event specialist with The Perfect Date (Tulsa, OK), who contributed her work pro bono for the L.A. event. "Instead of writing a release, sending it to reporters and hoping for traffic, PRWeb helped us reach the blogging community and other online sources that impact search engine optimization, which drives traffic to our projects."

The first press release drew 1,000 Facebook page views and earned 150 new Facebook fans within 24 hours. The second drove 1,400 page views in the first 24 hours, received nearly 60 retweets on Twitter and drove the event's Facebook fan count past 500.

"The first release created so much excitement among readers that they were looking forward to additional information," says Lawson, explaining why the second release was produced. She says an added benefit of online press releases is that "they stay on the Internet forever," rather than being tossed into a reporter's trash basket after the event ends.

Source: Cheryl Lawson, Founder, The Perfect Date, Tulsa, OK. Phone (478) 227-2789. E-mail: cheryl@theperfect-date.com. Website: www.theperfect-date.com

New Media Must-dos

When communicating via new social media venues, be sure to:

✓ Distribute press releases online. This allows you to embed multimedia content like video clips, creating a much more dynamic announcement.

✓ Contact bloggers as well as reporters. Search for those who write about what your organization does and put the bloggers' e-mail addresses on your press list.

✓ Measure success in people, not placements. These days, it's not so much about how many stories are generated around your event; it's about how many Facebook fans and Twitter followers you accrue as a result. Each is a tangible resource at your fingertips!

✓ Increase search engine optimization (SEO) to get your website listed at the top of the page in online searches.

Poll Audiences, Then Choose Social Media

Thinking of creating an organizational presence on a social networking site? Streamline your efforts by first polling your audiences to see which site they prefer, then focusing on the one or two most-popular sites first.

In April 2009, staff with College of the Mainland (Texas City, TX) posted a week-long poll on their home page asking users to choose the online social networking site they used most: Facebook, Flickr, MySpace, Twitter, YouTube or none.

"We wanted to see where we could do some potential advertising and where to reach our students and potential students on the Web," says Lana Pigao, director of marketing and publications. She notes that at the time, the only site the college used was Facebook.

Poll responses were recorded in a database and will be analyzed when the college creates its annual marketing plan and budget. Once that information is analyzed, staff will decide which other social networking options to pursue.

Pigao says the college chose to create an online poll instead of a traditional poll to add an interactive and fun element to their website.

The marketing and communications staff created poll questions, and the college webmaster used Poll Daddy (www.polldaddy.com), which offers free and paid accounts that allow users to create polls and surveys, to create the poll.

Source: Lana Pigao, Director of Marketing and Publications, College of the Mainland, Texas City, TX. Phone (409) 938-1211, ext. 434. E-mail: lpigao@com.edu

PULLING IT ALL TOGETHER: SOCIAL MEDIA STRATEGY

Three Reasons to Spend Time on Regular Online Networking

So you're sitting at your desk with a few minutes to spare. You open up your Facebook page. Guilty pleasure or smart business move?

Smart move, definitely, says Mandy Wittschen, feature article writer, Haley Marketing Group (Avon, OH): "I liken it to regular exercise. The more effort you put into your online networking, the greater the results you'll see."

Wittschen says the following three options are just a small portion of the opportunities that await you online.

1. **Positioning yourself as an expert** by writing and posting articles, sharing links to helpful content or answering a question. Make sure to include a link to your profile in your organization's online press room.

2. **Drawing traffic to your website or professional blog.** Wittschen says you can adjust your LinkedIn settings to automatically remind your contacts to come and see what's new.

3. **Taking advantage of viral marketing.** Facebook allows you to develop applications that sit on other people's profile pages where they can invite others to include the application on their own pages — all with no work from you. Brainstorm the best ways to use this feature for promoting your cause or organization.

While the possibilities for using online networks to promote your organization and its efforts are endless, your time is not. Wittschen recommends thoroughly researching networks, then focusing your efforts on one or two that best match your needs.

Source: Mandy Wittschen, Feature Article Writer, Haley Marketing Group, Avon, OH. Phone (888) 696-2900. E-mail: mwittschen000@centurytel.net

Make the Message Match the Audience

Staff at the Performing Arts Workshop (San Francisco, CA) rely on social networking options to communicate important information. Anne Trickey, program and communications coordinator, says she has worked to glean which groups in the organization's constituency respond best to particular types of messaging. She shares some of her findings, and how she uses that information to better match the message to its intended audience:

☐ **Facebook and other social media:** "In our July 2010 newsletter, we sent out a request for our entire database to become fans of (or Like) the Performing Arts Workshop on Facebook. We've found it's a good way to get immediate response; people can see pieces of information that give them a good feeling about what we do (and) immediately RSVP to events or comment on what we're doing. It may not be as beautiful to look at as an e-mail newsletter, but an e-mail takes more work to put together — it has to be structured and messaged as a whole. A Facebook post can be brief. Here, we reach a smaller donor base (and) they are most likely to take action on the Internet."

☐ **Traditional mail and word of mouth:** "Older donors respond best to this type of communication — which, in our case, is most of our donor base. These donors are more likely to get behind a campaign than the people who are plugged in to the Internet, so it's important to speak to them where they will hear it. For them, we focus on results and communicate youth outcomes — success stories from within the community. We involve site partners, schools and communities to communicate how the children are learning '21st century skills,

---

Seek Donated Video Services

For donated or inexpensive video, troll your community for start-up videography companies and producers seeking to build their portfolios, says Anne Trickey, program and communications coordinator for the Performing Arts Workshop (San Francisco, CA). "The people who put us in touch with our videographers were message-minded and familiar with the language that we use. It was easy to communicate that message to the videographers, and the end product — a combined development and communications effort — turned out really well. We got the product for free, and the videographers got a great example of their work."

---

creative expression and self efficacy.' That's our message. It mobilizes people."

☐ **YouTube:** "People who have seen our videos on YouTube tend to be outside of what we think of as our constituency, which is to say we haven't solicited them. But here, we are expanding our pool of supporters, which strengthens the organization." One of the biggest struggles for a group like theirs, she adds, is finding artists who are also great teachers "who understand what we want them to do, and are good in the classroom. When we attract artists who are really engaged in what we do, that gets results. And results attract donors."

Source: Anne Trickey, Program and Communications Coordinator, Performing Arts Workshop, San Francisco, CA. Phone (415) 673-2634 E-mail: anne@performingartsworkshop.org. Website: www.performingartsworkshop.org

PULLING IT ALL TOGETHER: SOCIAL MEDIA STRATEGY

Analyze Social Media Efforts to Measure Return On Investment

You begin by placing an important announcement on your organization's website. Next, you tweet a link to the announcement asking your Twitter followers to check it out. A few days later, you post a synopsis of the announcement on your blog, including a link to the original Web page. You might even send another tweet announcing the blog post.

And because you integrated Twitter into your LinkedIn and Facebook pages, additional fans, friends and contacts receive the news through those outlets.

Such cross-fertilization makes for good communication strategy while providing a body of concrete metrics to gauge the effectiveness of social media efforts, says David Sieg, vice president of strategic marketing, YourMembership.com, Inc. (St. Petersburg, FL).

Sieg says the following areas are particularly suited to measurement:

✓ **Inbound clicks.** The amount of traffic social media communications are driving to your website is an important measure of overall impact, says Sieg. How many users are clicking through to your site from your blog? From your Twitter tweets? From your Facebook page? Measure this information and use it.

✓ **Industry links.** Links are the mark of online relevance, and the number of industry groups and prominent bloggers who link to your website suggests the regard in which your organization (or at least its published content) is held, says Sieg.

✓ **Audience.** Whether friends or fans, subscribers or followers, your loyal audience members are another easily tabulated metric. But Sieg cautions that readership is only a first step, and that user-initiated interaction — filling out a contact page, downloading a contact form, reposting your article — should be the primary goal.

✓ **Search engine optimization.** Your organization's organic page rank (the place it appears on a search engine's page of unpaid search results) is a matter of great importance, says Sieg. Not only does it reflect the number of people viewing your content and linking to your posts, it determines how easily potential members will be able to find your online presence. Never ignore a rising or falling page rank.

✓ **Website analytics.** Google Analytics (www.google.com/analytics), the gold standard of free website analysis,

Build Workable Social Media Strategy

While social media is new territory for many membership organizations, its underlying strategy is not as foreign as some might imagine, says David Sieg, vice president of strategic marketing, YourMembership.com, Inc. (St. Petersburg, FL).

"Start a social media strategy by defining a concrete goal — a membership level, dollar figure, etc. — that is quantifiable and has a relatively short-term end date, maybe a year to 18 months," Sieg says.

The next step, he says, is devising objectives, both social and traditional, that further this goal. "If your goal is achieving X number of members by 2012, you might say you will send Y direct mail pieces, launch a social media marketing campaign via Twitter and LinkedIn, and commit Z dollars to advertising."

Finally, devise operational tactics supporting each objective. This planning process must include development of a defined content strategy.

"Firing random thoughts out across Twitter will not get the job done," says Sieg. "You need a consistent voice, a consistent message and a consistency of communication across many kinds of media. An annual schedule of communication, detailing by quarter or month what will be sent out to whom by what portal, is an invaluable part of any social media initiative."

can determine many of the previous metrics including clicks, links and referring sites. Website usage patterns revealed by online analytics (e.g., how long users view any particular page, what pages users leave your website from, what percentage of users landing on a contact page complete the form) also give clues about user preferences and behavior.

Finally, Sieg says, don't ignore conventional metrics. "Is your membership growing? Is your revenue increasing? Are your services being utilized? These are areas social media should be having an impact on and should, therefore, constitute another form of measurement."

Source: David Sieg, Vice President, Strategic Marketing, YourMembership.com, Inc., St. Petersburg, FL. Phone (727) 827-0046. E-mail: dsieg@yourmembership.com. Website: www.yourmembership.com

PULLING IT ALL TOGETHER: SOCIAL MEDIA STRATEGY

Use Social Media as an Effective Marketing Tool

An important first step in creating effective social media connections is to talk about social media marketing, not just social media, says David Sieg, vice president of strategic marketing at YourMembership.com, Inc. (St. Petersburg, FL). "Social media is a new and quickly evolving trend, but its value lies in very traditional marketing goals like raising revenue and growing membership," Sieg says. "Organizations need to make sure that focus on marketing isn't lost in a sea of fans and tweets."

Here Sieg answers three common questions about social media marketing.

Which social media platforms produce the most consistent results?

"I recommend Twitter as a first focus, followed by LinkedIn and Facebook as a distant third. Services that can augment social media marketing include Flickr (www.flickr.com) for sharing photos, YouTube for sharing videos, and organizational blogs."

Where should our blog be hosted? As part of the organizational website? As a stand-alone site?

"We do a lot of work with search engine optimization and have found the best approach to be a WordPress (www.wordpress.org) blog installed on your website and hosted internally. This is a free application that is very flexible in look and feel and very good at getting indexed by search engines."

What kind of tone should we use in social media communications?

"Ironically, one of the biggest mistakes we see is organizations being too social with social media. If your president wants to talk about local sports teams on his or her personal blog, that's fine, but organizational communications need to be focused on conveying useful information and unique insight."

Source: David Sieg, Vice President, Strategic Marketing, YourMembership.com, Inc., St. Petersburg, FL. Phone (727) 827-0046. E-mail: dsieg@yourmembership.com. Website: www.yourmembership.com

Giving up Control Vital to Viral Campaigns

In today's tech-savvy world, word travels fast. And when your supporters start texting and tweeting about your special event or fundraiser, then their friends forward that news to their friends, the campaign has gone viral.

"Giving in to serendipity is part of the entire concept of going viral," says Nonprofit Consultant Ken Goldstein of Goldstein Consulting (Los Gatos, CA). "If a campaign is driven from top-down, with a command and control attitude that was approved in endless closed-door meetings, then by definition it's not viral, no matter how popular or successful it may be."

To be truly viral, Goldstein says, a campaign must be person-to-person sharing out of true interest, "not carefully orchestrated, scheduled and monitored organization-to-masses distribution." Unfortunately, he says this troubles many professional fundraisers and their boards of directors because the very things that make something viral also prevent it from being put in a budget with any accuracy.

The concept of going viral is not new. As long as there have been nonprofits, there have been people-driven efforts to support them, from bake sales to asking for donations in lieu of birthday gifts. "The difference in the social media age is scale," he says. "Instead of supporters bringing in a few hundred dollars from the couple of dozen people they are in physical contact with, the message is quickly forwarded electronically to friends of friends of friends, and the results

can be huge."

All nonprofits should be prepared for a fundraising effort, publicity campaign or other communications element to go viral, Goldstein says. To do so, he advises:

- Truly engage friends and followers with social media. "That means being on Facebook and Twitter with regularly posted updates, including photos of your events and good deeds. You don't just post and run. You listen to what they're saying, and you reply swiftly. Social media is not a broadcast medium; it's a conversation platform."

- Have a large, easy-to-find "Donate Now" button on every page of your website.

- Make your website accessible and easy to read (and donate) from mobile devices. "This includes phones, iPads and whatever is invented next week," says Goldstein.

- Think phones. If your message goes viral, bringing people to your website, and it's not maximized to be read on a phone, and doesn't have a call to action front and center, he says, "You've just blown your opportunity."

Source: Ken Goldstein, Goldstein Consulting. E-mail: ken@goldstein.net

Social Media Strategies That Increase Visibility

Far from being a passing fad, social media is rapidly extending its way into the corporate and nonprofit sectors and changing the way stakeholders communicate with each other, and how they expect to communicate with your organization.

What is social media? It is using the Internet to instantly collaborate, share information and have a conversation about ideas, causes and organizations we care about powered by social media tools (e.g., social networking sites, blogs, podcasts, etc.).

Holly Ross, executive director, NTEN: The Nonprofit Technology Network (Portland, OR), says nonprofit communicators must understand how social media's newfound popularity will impact their cause and relay that to their constituency.

"As nonprofits, we're used to being authorities to our communities," Ross says. "Our role has been to decide what's important regarding our issues, to tell our community what matters and to organize them to create change."

But the development of the Internet has forced nonprofits to change how they relate to their communities, she says: "First, the Internet has made accessing information incredibly easy. If you want to know about logging in your state, Google will tell you what's going on. Second (and this is the newest part), the Internet has made it ridiculously easy for us to share that information with each other, and to organize around that information.

"What that means is that people don't need us to tell them what matters. They don't need us to organize them. So as nonprofits our value proposition has shifted. We need to learn how they are using these tools to organize themselves, and what they are saying about our issues so we can understand what value we can bring to them."

Ross emphasizes that nonprofit communicators should think of social media as a series of steps that must be taken to increase visibility:

1. **Listen and participate in conversations that are already happening.** First, find out and listen to what people are talking about regarding the issues about which you care. How are they talking about the issues? What's motivating them? Next, use that knowledge to share your own insights and resources.

2. **Share your story.** Once you have a feel for the conversation, get your own story out there via blogs, podcasts, videos, etc. and invite the community to participate. Be brave and create content that is appropriate for your audiences and encourages feedback and conversation.

3. **Generate buzz.** Use sites like Facebook, StumbleUpon, Digg and Twitter to tell the world about what you're doing. Build a community of peers on these sites that will help you get the word out about your stories to their networks.

"The key to all these is community," says Ross. "You have to build real relationships with real people to make it work. That means that you'll have to contribute as much as you take, and you'll have to be open to whatever the community wants to tell you."

Source: Holly Ross, Executive Director, NTEN: The Nonprofit Technology Network, Portland, OR. Phone (415) 397-9000. E-mail: holly@nten.org

---

Social Media's Challenges

Like many forms of communication, social media has its pros and cons, says Holly Ross, executive director, NTEN: The Nonprofit Technology Network (Portland, OR).

Ross offers an example of how social media has changed communications for the better in terms of speed and scope: "We always wanted to create that perfect viral e-mail that would get forwarded around the Web. Adding 25 people to an e-mail send list is tedious compared to adding a link to Digg (www.digg.com). Getting your networks to tell a friend is all about capitalizing on their emotions in the moment. The easier that is, the more you'll get out of it. And social media makes it very easy."

While social media has helped in this manner, she notes it isn't a panacea. Its pitfalls include:

✓ **Presenting challenges to an organization's many cultures.** "To successfully implement a social media strategy, your organization must be prepared to behave in new ways. You have to be much more open and transparent than many organizations have been up to this point. The idea of accepting comments on a blog is abhorrent to many organizations, for example. They can't bear the idea of someone saying something negative."

✓ **Lack of control.** "The biggest mistake I see organizations make is the attempt to control their social media strategy too much. That's not how social media works. You can't delete negative comments. You have to respond to them honestly and openly."

✓ **Social media structure vs. organizational structure.** "We're used to working in departmental silos; program does program work, fundraising raises money, marketing tells our stories. Social media combine elements of all of those.... The folks implementing social media strategies are crossing departments more frequently, challenging our old ways of getting work done."

PULLING IT ALL TOGETHER: SOCIAL MEDIA STRATEGY

Formulate and Publicize Social Media Guidelines

Well-crafted social media guidelines foster openness and encourage growth while establishing what is appropriate for that organization.

Heidi Sullivan, vice president of media research for Cision (Chicago, IL), says, "Whether your organization has committed to a social media presence yet or not, it's now readily apparent that it should establish guidelines that spell out the rules and standards of online engagement and behavior."

Many organizations post social media codes of conduct on their websites. To begin crafting yours, see what others are doing, or start from scratch and create a set of guidelines that reflect the nature and needs of your organization.

Sullivan, who has studied and developed a variety of social media policies, says these are her five best practices.

❑ **Think like a spokesperson.** Every employee with a Facebook page or Twitter account essentially becomes a spokesperson for your organization. Your policy for employees should include the same limitations and guidelines your official spokesperson has about what they can and can't reveal about the company.

❑ **Designate representatives.** For your official social media sites, decide who your representatives are and give them limitations on their personal social media involve-

ment. Other staff can be personally involved with social media but should not identify themselves with your company or brand.

❑ **Avoid jargon.** Use language employees and volunteers can understand.

❑ **Identify off-limit subjects.** The more specific you are, the easier your policy is to enforce. Do not assume everyone knows what is controversial for your agency.

❑ **Open a discussion.** Bring your employees into the planning process.

Finally, Sullivan says, don't forget the word social in social media. Removing personality or opinion from these sites is not possible, and should not be your goal. However, with a little controlled messaging and a few guidelines, you can foster growth through social media without risking embarrassment or worse from an employee or volunteer.

Cision offers a social media guidelines white paper that is available for download at http://us.cision.com/campaigns/2009_sm_policy/request.asp.

Source: Heidi Sullivan, Vice President, Media Research, CISION US, INC., Chicago, IL. Phone (312) 873-6653. E-mail: Heidi.Sullivan@cision.com. Website: http://us.cision.com/index.asp

---

Social Media Criteria to Get You Started on Your Policy

Social media guidelines that Heidi Sullivan, vice president of media research, developed for her employer, Cision (Chicago, IL), include:

Social sites are public. Use common sense. Presume that even if you don't identify yourself as a Cision employee, information on the Web will make you identifiable.

If you identify yourself, be professional. If you choose to include Cision as your employer in your bio or profile on a social site, conduct yourself professionally there.

Embrace your personality. Be yourself and feel free to say what is on your mind, but do so respectfully.

Be nice. Don't vent, bash or poke fun at people, businesses, companies, brands, competitors or geographical locations. Think before posting and when in doubt, don't hit "send."

Don't sell. Identify opportunities, but social networking sites are not venues for your sales pitch.

Mind the competitors. Watch them, but don't harass them. Follow them, but do not republish their message.

Be the first to respond to your own mistakes. If you make an error, be up front about your mistake and correct it quickly.

Protect confidential information and proprietary information. Social computing blurs traditional boundaries between internal and external communications. Be mindful of the difference.

Don't forget your day job. Make sure that online activities do not interfere with your job.

PULLING IT ALL TOGETHER: SOCIAL MEDIA STRATEGY

Online Tools Monitor What Others Are Saying About You

How can you know when and how to engage in social media dialogue unless you're aware of the conversation in the first place?

The easiest way to get plugged in to the online chatter is to track it using various social media monitoring tools.

Heidi Sullivan, vice-president of media research for Cision (Chicago, IL), says such tools "give you real time insights about what's being said, by whom, about you, your products or your industry. They enable you to react appropriately to conversations, and evaluate the effectiveness of your response."

Here are some free sites to start with:

❑ www.google.com/alerts or www.blogsearch.google.com — Choose your keywords and the sites e-mail you when these keywords are used in online articles or blogs. These sites are a great tool for communication managers who want to ensure they are being correctly quoted by journalists. When something is wrong, you know immediately, and it only takes a phone call to set the record straight.

❑ www.search.twitter.com — This is similar to Google services but does not require an account. You would need to schedule time to check the site for an up-to-the-minute account of what real people are twittering to each other about your organization.

❑ www.keotag.com — With this hybrid of the above-listed sites, you start with one keyword and then search Google, Twitter, BlogSpot and others. This can be a real timesaver.

❑ www.netvibes.com — Using this most advanced of the free social monitoring sites, you create a dashboard personalized to your agency and follow dozens of blogs, activity streams and Twitter conversations. The site allows you to share the dashboard with clients or volunteers.

Once you start monitoring social media, use the information to manage your reputation as an individual or agency, measure campaigns' effectiveness and improve your overall public relations message.

Source: Heidi Sullivan, Vice President, Media Research, CISION US, INC., Chicago, IL. Phone (312) 873-6653. E-mail: Heidi.Sullivan@cision.com. Website: http://us.cision.com

Link to Social Media Networks

In today's technologically savvy world, tweeting isn't just for the birds.

Even members of Congress use social media like Twitter.com to stay in touch with constituents in real time, sending brief text messages (called tweeting) that can be viewed on the Internet, cell phones and on other portable communications devices.

Facebook, LinkedIn, Flickr and YouTube are just a few of the free online social media sites where you can create an account or group to communicate with existing volunteers and recruit new ones.

To put these social networking tools to use promoting your special event, increase your organization's online presence and boost awareness of your mission:

❑ **Start a Facebook group about your event.** Once you have recruited or identified supporters who already use Facebook, you can send invitations to meetings, post photo albums, give daily progress reports about completed tasks and advertise jobs that still need to be done.

❑ **Tweet messages to spread news.** Your committee meeting has been canceled, but you can't call everyone in time. Twitter allows you to log on to your account and spread the word to many users at once, who can in turn notify others of the change in plans.

❑ **Launch a photo album and blog on Flickr.** Some of your volunteers have traveled to Africa on behalf of your organization. Start an account where they can post photos, write about their activities and share links to news with those at home.

❑ **Study social media options for the best fit.** Chances are that many of your volunteers already have accounts on LinkedIn, Twitter, Facebook, YouTube or Flickr. Most of these sites link to each other, so news you share can have a positive ripple effect. Portal websites, like www.socialmediaanswers.com, give tutorials on how to build and cultivate your own network, and describe the benefits of the most popular and versatile services.

Social Media and Communications Technology

TECHNOLOGY TO ENHANCE REAL-WORLD EVENTS

Online communication becomes more important with every passing day, but real-world events are still the bread and butter of most nonprofits. Whether it is mobile phone applications that enhance an annual convention, social media platforms that boost attendance at a major fundraiser or internet services that simplify coordination and logistics, the following ideas will help your event be everything you need it to be.

Use Social Networking to Maximize Special Event Success

Looking to use social networking to promote your event? Plan your steps for doing so to best use precious planning time and best utilize these growing communication venues.

Both Mandi Mueller, public relations coordinator of Special Olympics Missouri (Jefferson City, MO), and Jennifer Bohac, director of the Texas A&M Association of Former Students' Traveling Aggies program (College City, TX), agree: The biggest downside to social networking sites is the time they can eat up.

The key to using social networking in promoting special events or other aspects of your organization, they say, is focusing on what clearly works for your organization.

For Mueller, maintaining that focus in the face of a Twitter account and five separate Facebook pages can be a challenge. But most of her work goes toward one popular effort — a page (linked to the Twitter account) hosted by Shiver Bear, the polar bear mascot of Special Olympics Missouri's largest fundraising event, the Polar Bear Plunge.

"Shiver sends out status updates, posts photos from events and invites people to activities," she says. "He's the face of events. Things mean more coming from him than they would from me or other staff members."

The updates Mueller sends on behalf of Shiver every day could include details about upcoming events, articles featuring Special Olympics or volunteer needs, but she stresses that they nearly always include a clickable link. "I don't want people to just read something," she says. "The point is for them to do something, to take action."

Mueller also emphasizes that regular, daily communication is crucial to building a fan base that is actively involved.

Though Special Olympics Missouri maintains a cause page that can raise money directly, Mueller currently prefers to channel new contacts toward traditional fundraisers. To do this, she has found that placing ads on Facebook is effective.

With the personal information available on Facebook, she says, "You can drill down by people's age, gender, hobbies, alma mater, current location — almost anything you can imagine. I don't know anywhere else advertising can be that focused."

In 2008, Mueller says, she spent $277 on an ad that was viewed almost 1.15 million times. Out of that, 424 people clicked through for more information on the fundraiser it promoted. "It's only a click-through rate of about .037 percent, but if even half those 424 people pay $50 to register, it can really add up," she says.

The Traveling Aggies are much newer to the social networking scene but are already seeing benefits, says Bohac. Foremost among these is the ability to give real-time updates in multiple formats. On campus she may only send updates once a week, but while accompanying a tour overseas she can send live text messages, photos and even video clips straight from her Blackberry.

"This includes participants in action as it's happening," Bohac says. "Not having to wait until the trip is done, they feel personally involved. It creates buzz and gets people thinking about maybe taking a trip of their own."

Bohac appreciates having a way to communicate fast-changing details without a long stream of e-mails, but highlights a more bottom-line benefit to social networking as well. "It's cheap! As schools and other organizations feel the budget pinch, we just can't do as much with mailings. This is one more way to keep in contact with the people we serve."

Sources: Jennifer Bohac, Director of Travel Program, Association of Former Students, Texas A&M University, College Station, TX. Phone (979) 845-7514. E-mail: Jbohac87@aggienetwork.com Mandi Mueller, Public Relations Coordinator, Special Olympics Missouri Jefferson City, MO. Phone (800) 846-2682. E-mail: Mueller@somo.org

Upgrade Your Social Networking

If you frequently Twitter to members and donors, a new generation of electronic tools can save them time and give you a wealth of valuable information.

A service called bit.ly, for example, not only shortens URLs to a tweet-friendly 10 characters, it tracks how many times people click through to embedded links, says Mandi Mueller, public relations coordinator at Special Olympics Missouri (Jefferson City, MO), who uses the service. Knowing this information makes it easy to assess members' interest in various photos, news links and updates.

Bit.ly and similar tools like tr.im (another URL shortening service) are available for free download. Plug either term or the phrase "URL shortening service" into your favorite Internet search engine to learn more.

Social Media and Communications Technology

TECHNOLOGY TO ENHANCE REAL-WORLD EVENTS

Online Calendars Ease Planning, Offer Ready Access

Online calendars are useful for event planning, allowing quick changes and updates at each stage while creating an up-to-the-minute glance from any Internet-linked computer.

Many online calendars can also be linked to your existing website, plus let you send e-mail or text messages.

Also, many online calendars are free.

Visit the websites listed at right to begin identifying the right calendar for your event.

Online Calendar Links

- Google (www.google.com/calendar)
- Bravenet (www.bravenet.com/webtools/calendar/)
- Cozi (www.cozi.com)
- Yahoo! (www.calendar.yahoo.com)
- WORKetc (www.worketc.com)

Phone Application Aids Event Planning

Event planning applications can help you plan important elements straight from your handheld phone. Depending on the type of SmartPhone you use, applications can offer event budget calculators, meeting space calculators and event scheduling possibilities.

According to Phone magazine, nearly 173.6 million SmartPhone units were sold in 2008 alone. Nearly 17 percent of mobile phone subscribers own SmartPhones, up from 11 percent in 2008, says CNET.com.

Recently released event planning apps allow users to determine the comfortable number of guests for any given event, calculate the budgetary needs of each event based on the number of guests, determine the steps needed to effectively plan the event and keep planners on task with scheduling components.

Mobile Applications Maximize Meeting Effectiveness

Smartphone applications are popping up regularly at membership organizations' annual meetings and conventions, and behind every one is someone like Cameron Bishop, CEO of Ascend Integrated Media (Overland Park, KS). Here, Bishop answers questions about the technical side of developing a mobile application:

Are there different kinds of mobile apps or just functions?

"The two big categories are native applications specifically designed for and downloaded onto a phone, and web-based applications called WAPs."

To what extent are conference applications useful beyond the event itself?

"Apps stay live after the convention ends, so they have tremendous capacity for further usage. Many people continue using our applications for nothing more than basic news and weather feeds, so the potential for ongoing communication is there to be exploited. The biggest obstacle is really limitations in organizations' own thinking."

What is the time frame and cost for developing a mobile app?

"You want the app to be live a minimum of 30 days prior to the event so attendees can download it. Development generally takes around two months, so three to four months is sufficient for the actual development process. But the more aggressively an application is marketed, the more widely it will be used, so beginning promotion six or seven months out will raise your download and usage rates exponentially.

"For an application with a wide range of functionality running on all platforms, the general range would be $10,000 to $20,000."

What should organizations be wary of in app developers?

"Make sure their product runs equally well across all mobile platforms.... Many developers cut their teeth on iPhones and are most comfortable with them, so the applications they develop work on Blackberries or Androids but don't have the same degree of functionality or graphic appearance."

What opportunities for revenue generation do mobile apps offer?

"Banner and tower ads are the most common digital sponsorship opportunities, but the whole application can be sponsored by a single company, with its branding appearing throughout. If you have an exhibit guide as part of the app, you can sell upgrades to enhanced listings like links to video or audio podcasts, digital flipbooks or PDFs. Text-message based advertising is another option."

What do you wish organizations knew about the process of developing a mobile app?

"Many organizations don't plan for the work needed to create content for the app. They often have not stopped to think about who is going to write the content for the news feed or format the data for the exhibitor guide. Similarly, all applications have some capacity for monetization, but someone needs to sell that digital real estate. Organizations need to have people to fill those rolls or be willing to pay a developer to do it for them."

Source: Cameron Bishop, CEO, Ascend Integrated Media, Overland Park, KS. Phone (816) 591-6610. E-mail: Cbishop@ascendmedia.com. Website: www.ascendintegratedmedia.com

TECHNOLOGY TO ENHANCE REAL-WORLD EVENTS

Blogs Reveal Fresh Angles On Special Event Planning

For fresh ideas for your event, check out some of the many event planning blogs.

Here is just a sampling of event planning blogs that you can follow for ideas and advice for your next event-planning venture:

- **Cvent Meetings & Events** — http://blog.cvent.com/ blog/cvent — Established in 1999, this site specializes in event management and Web survey solutions, and features a plethora of event topics.

- **Unique Venues** — http://blog.uniquevenues.com/ — This site is designed to advise meeting and event planners in North America on locating interesting and unusual

venues with a database of more than 1,300 members.

- **Event Industry Thoughts** — http://eventplanning. typepad.com/ — This down-to-earth blog offers straightforward advice on the advances and trends in corporate event planning.

- **The Savvy Event** — http://thesavvyevent.blogspot.com — This blog offers tips on doing it yourself and videos to show you how.

- **Next Generation Event** — http://www. nextgenerationevent.com/greenevents/ — This event planning blog focuses on content, community and collaboration. Look for heartfelt, fresh ideas here.

Facilitate Member Conventions With a Mobile Application

Business professionals are increasingly treating mobile phones as a primary source of information — and expecting that others do the same. This is one reason staff at the Newspaper Association of America (Arlington, VA) produced a mobile phone application specifically for their annual mediaXchange conference.

"The application provided convenient and up-to-date access to most information contained in the onsite program guide," says Kevin McCourt, vice president of advertising and exhibition sales. "The conference program, speaker and session outlines, roster of exhibitors, hotel information, and a live Twitter and blog feed with ongoing posts were all delivered to pretty much any mobile device available."

Though much of the information was available on a dedicated website, navigating it was far easier in a native mobile application than a phone-based web browser, says McCourt.

Because the application was new to the 2010 conference, organizers made it easy to acquire, having members text a short code to a five-digit number to receive a website and instructions on how to download and install the application,

or download directly at the conference website.

Reaction to the application was uniformly enthusiastic, says McCourt. Usage statistics showed almost 50 percent of event participants using the application, with an average of more than 40 interactions per user and a 25 percent clickthrough rate to more information on sessions, speakers or exhibitors.

A conference survey identified the application as the second-most frequently used tool (after the conference website) in planning for and participating in the event.

While the application was developed as an in-kind service from corporate sponsors, McCourt estimates its market value at $20,000. Mobile software developer Handmark, Inc. (Kansas City, MO) conceived and delivered the application in about 90 days.

When developing a mobile application, McCourt advises starting early to ensure time for testing and tweaking it prior to your launch date.

Source: Kevin McCourt, Vice President of Advertising and Exhibition Sales, Newspaper Association of America. Arlington, VA. Phone (571) 366-1055. E-mail: mccourt@naa.org

Use E-Invitations to Save Costs, Expedite Your Message

One of the simplest and most cost-effective ways to save on your event planning budget is to eliminate paper invitations and replace them with e-invitations. E-invitations require no mailing labels, stamps or envelopes.

E-invitations can replace an event invitation or can be used to compliment one. If your next event still requires the mailing of an invitation, use an e-invitation as a follow-up reminder to the hard copy that was mailed. Doing so will

ensure guests will still receive an invitation even if the hard copy gets lost in the mail.

Here are five websites that offer free e-invitations:

- www.evite.com
- www.sendomatic.com
- www.mypunchbowl.com
- www.smilebox.com
- www.invite-o-matic.com

Social Media and Communications Technology

TECHNOLOGY TO ENHANCE REAL-WORLD EVENTS

Message Boards Give Voice to Alumni

Barbara Bessmer Henry, director of alumni relations, Oglethorpe University (Atlanta, GA), says their alumni had a voice online long before the advent of Facebook, through the university's message boards. Henry does note, however, that traffic on those boards has definitely slowed down since social networking sites have surged in popularity. In spite of that, they won't be abandoning their online community any time soon. Henry says it still serves a very distinct purpose for them.

The message boards are extremely beneficial in preparation for the annual faculty appreciation reception held during alumni weekend. "Our faculty/student ratio is very low, which is a huge selling point for us. Students build strong connections with the faculty," says Henry. "We use the message boards to get quotes from alumni about faculty that we can use in PowerPoint messages during the reception. Faculty is the one hot point that people will continue to comment on over time."

Henry says the way the software is set up also works as a reminder for those who haven't yet made their own comments, pulling new comments to the top, which piques people's interest. "They say, 'Hey, I should do that!'"

Other hot topics include Love at First Sight on the Quad, where alumni can share the story of how they fell in love

---

Should Social Networking Sites Replace Existing Online Communities?

Barbara Bessmer Henry, director of alumni relations at Oglethorpe University (Atlanta, GA), says social networking sites have totally changed the way her staff and other member-based organizations work. In doing so, she says, some institutions are leaving their original online communities and online message boards behind.

That may be shortsighted, she says.

"All of our event registrations are handled online through that system," says Henry. "As a result, all of the information we need is at our disposal. We are able to use that and download it to create name tags and other materials for our events. It's like having an extra half staff person on board. Some information is just not applicable on sites like Facebook."

---

at Oglethorpe and What are you reading? Henry says she and her staff also use stories from the message boards in Oglethorpe's other publications, when appropriate.

Source: Barbara Bessmer Henry, Director of Alumni Relations, Oglethorpe University, Atlanta, GA. Phone (404) 364-8443. E-mail: bhenry@Oglethorpe.edu

---

Websites, Software Cater to Electronic Invitations

For help designing, sending or managing invitations for your event, try these websites and software options that include tools geared specifically for nonprofit event management:

✓ **Blacktie Colorado (www.blacktie-colorado.com), Denver, CO**, has a mission of empowering nonprofit organizations "by providing access to online event planning and convenient, easy, one-stop, Web-based technology for heightening awareness, raising money, managing events, communicating with supporters and managing critical data." Online event management software can be customized using more than 35 proprietary planning tools.

✓ **Paperless Post (www.paperlesspost.com), New York, NY**, is a website that works like an online stationery store and is geared toward individual customers. Many for-profits and nonprofits alike swear by the striking beauty of Paperless Post's e-mailable invitations when the main goal is to make a good first impression. Designed to look like a sophisticated, paper-made card — complete with a traditional envelope that opens onscreen — these electronic invitations can be customized with photos, logos and more.

✓ **Campaigner (www.campaigner.com), by Protus (Ottawa, Ontario, Canada)** is a Software as a Service (SaaS) business communications service that works with small businesses and nonprofits, offering them various e-mail marketing and promotional tools, including those for special events. Design your electronic invitation, send it, then track who opens your e-mails, clicks through to your website, replies, etc. Campaigner is praised by clients for its usability, helpful features and reliable customer service. Sign up for a 30-day free trial, then move on to a monthly paid service plan.

✓ **Small Act (www.smallact.com), Washington, D.C.**, is a software and consulting company that works exclusively with nonprofits, including Miriam's Kitchen (Washington, D.C.), a homeless services provider; Kaboom! (Washington, D.C.) which builds playgrounds for children in needy areas; and the Epilepsy Foundation of Florida (Miami, FL). Small Act places a strong emphasis on social media, while its Thrive software is heralded by clients for allowing invites to be composed and tracked online in one central location.

Social Media and Communications Technology: Essential Strategies for Nonprofits and Associations.
Edited by Scott C. Stevenson.
© 2011 Stevenson, Inc. Published 2011 by Stevenson, Inc.

Social Media and Communications Technology

VIRTUAL MEETINGS AND DISTANCE SOLUTIONS

Do you have clients, suppliers or partners in other parts of the country? Board members who are frequently out of town? Staff members or consultants working off-site? The search for top talent often transcends geography, and when it does, tools to facilitate collaboration at a distance become essential. The following suggestions offer ways to get the most from your far-flung group — without getting them together in the same room.

How to Implement a Successful Virtual Meeting

Virtual meetings electronically connect partners, clients and associates from any location while saving on gas and travel costs.

Jim Bandy, president, Brainband Technology Services (Dallas, TX), offers points to keep in mind to make your online meeting effective:

1. **Choose a program that fits your needs.** Popular virtual meeting platforms available for purchase include Microsoft Office Live Meeting, Adobe ConnectNow and Cisco WebEx. Free software such as Mikogo and FreeConferenceCalls incorporates webinar capabilities. Bandy says the program you choose should have a few key features:

   ✓ **Whiteboard** — This feature allows the presenter to edit documents and other materials as in a traditional meeting, letting attendees see markups in real time.

   ✓ **Chat** — This tool could display messages for everyone to see or show private instant messages between two people, allowing attendees to communicate with the presenter and other participants without interrupting the meeting's flow.

   ✓ **Control transfer** — In online meetings, it will be useful for the presenter to be able to transfer mouse and keyboard control to another team member in case further explanation is needed.

2. **Do a run-through.** "People respect a well-run meeting, so become familiar with the tools and applications in your online conference software beforehand in order to avoid embarrassing moments," says Bandy. Plan details, including scheduling the meeting at a convenient time for everyone (keep time zones in mind) and planning a brief time for questions and answers.

3. **Don't over-invite.** Keep the invitation list short and only notify those whose attendance is mandatory. Send invitations well enough in advance and send a reminder the day before to ensure a prompt start. "Gathering the right people as opposed to the largest crowd will make your meeting more effective and increase the attentiveness and interaction in the meeting," says Bandy.

4. **Send an e-mail.** Sending a well-written e-mail will remind participants of the upcoming meeting and give them an idea about topics to be covered. When composing your e-mail, keep these things in mind: make the subject line attention grabbing; keep the copy conversational; and call out the benefits of the meeting and how it will serve the attendees. Also, be sure the time zone associated with the scheduled online meeting time is made clear in the e-mail. The end of the e-mail should include a call to action, motivating recipients to RSVP.

5. **Keep it interesting.** Spend the majority of the meeting interacting with attendees and sharing information of interest and benefit to all participants. Don't waste time on objectives that can be accomplished via e-mail or a phone call. Collaborate as a group on brainstorming, decision-making, team building, etc. Incorporating slides from Microsoft PowerPoint and documents from Microsoft Word or Excel helps break up the routine of a lecture and keep people visually focused.

Source: Jim Bandy, President, Brainband Technology Services, Dallas, TX. Phone (972) 231-7128. E-mail: jbandy@brainband.com

Teleseminars Educate Members

The Association of Ghostwriters (Fairport, NY) is a new online organization that offers members a wealth of information and resources through its website (www.associationofghostwriters.org). One of the major benefits, according to Marcia Layton Turner, founder and executive director, is access to monthly teleseminars.

Layton Turner offers tips for securing noteworthy speakers for teleseminars:

✓ Evaluate the biggest challenges your members face and locate experts who can address those issues effectively.

✓ Approach experts well in advance of your desired teleseminar date to increase odds they will be available.

✓ Highlight the size of your membership when seeking speakers. The larger your potential audience, the more interested your speakers will be.

✓ As teleseminars can be attended by anyone who has a phone, do not limit yourself to local speakers. Layton Turner recently welcomed Stacy Brice, founder of AssistU (Cockeysville, MD), which helps train and refer virtual assistants, as part of a call on how writers and ghostwriters can use virtual assistants to get more writing done.

Source: Marcia Layton Turner, Executive Director, Association of Ghostwriters, Fairport, NY. Phone (585) 586-8660. E-mail: info@associationofghostwriters.org. Website: www.associationofghostwriters.org

Virtual Board Meetings Allow Board to Address Timely Issues

Many organizations host virtual board meetings to save time and money or to communicate about issues in a more timely manner than face-to-face meetings.

The Association of College and Research Libraries (ACRL), a division of the American Library Association (Chicago, IL), which has 14 board members across the country, holds virtual board meetings as needed. Recent virtual meetings included two full board meetings in the last year and six meetings of the board's working groups. The full board meets face-to-face three times a year and the executive committee convenes twice more.

Katie Coombes, program officer for governance, says virtual board meetings allow them to address issues in a timely manner and advance priority projects much more quickly than when they did not meet virtually.

"While we are organized and plan for the future," Coombes says, "external timelines and opportunities can be met with a virtual board meeting more effectively than delaying the board action until the next scheduled meeting or incurring the added cost of an additional face-to-face meeting."

ACRL officials have tried a variety of virtual meeting software, including:

✓ The free Web collaboration tool, Dimdim (www.dimdim. com).

✓ Adobe Connect Pro (www.adobe.com/products/acrobat-connectpro/), which Coombes says cost under $1,000.

✓ iLinc (www.ilinc.com), which Coombes says the ALA's parent organization, the Association of College and Research Libraries recently purchased.

"We have limited ourselves to browser-based services to eliminate the need for board members to purchase or install software, as it would likely pose challenges and inconvenience for them," says Coombes.

All that is needed to participate is a USB headset, she says.

Coombes says they did not need to alter their bylaws in order to allow the board to conduct virtual meetings since they conform to the existing open meeting policy by posting the agenda and minutes.

In the virtual meetings, "We follow the same rules of order — the Sturgis Parliamentary Procedure," she says. "The main difference is that the virtual meeting software keeps all board members focused on the same document. This has helped some discussions.

"Virtual meetings are also much shorter than our face-to-face meetings," Coombes notes, "because they focus on a single issue rather than the laundry list that can build for face-to-face meetings."

Source: Katie Coombes, Program Officer, Association of College and Research Libraries, American Library Association, Chicago, IL. Phone (312) 280-2519. E-mail: kcoombes@ala.org

Weigh Pros, Cons of Skype

Skype (www.skype.com) is an online software application by Skype Technologies S.A. (Luxembourg) that lets registered users make phone calls through an Internet connection rather than traditional landlines or cell phones.

Calls from one Skype user to another are free for both parties. Skype users pay a fee when calling a landline or cell phone. Skype also offers instant messaging, video conferencing and file sharing, free when conducted between Skype users.

Representatives of two nonprofits that have switched to Skype — Lee Gimpel, board member at James River Writers (Richmond, VA), and Marty Guise, executive director, Lay Renewal Ministries (St. Louis, MO) — share its pros and cons:

Pros:

✓ Saving money. "We went from about $100 per month to about $200 per year" after switching from traditional phone use to Skype, Gimpel says.

✓ Cutting travel and other costs. "We have three board members out of eight who live out of state," Guise says. "While we still want to have annual, in-person meetings, the cost for others to travel is too much. In addition, one of our board members is not physically able to travel."

✓ Telecommuting. Gimpel says the organization's administrative director can use the Skype service at home and other out-of-office locations to make work-related calls at no additional cost.

Cons:

✓ Losing your old phone number.

✓ Caller ID issues. Gimpel says the person receiving a call made with Skype does not see a caller ID display that identifies the organization or location.

✓ Connection issues. "Two of the three (long-distance board members) did not call in advance to test their Skype systems," says Guise, and "one person was unable to use it. I would strongly advocate running several tests prior to having an official meeting."

Sources: Lee Gimpel, board member, James River Writers, Richmond, VA. Phone (804) 433-3790.
E-mail: info@jamesriverwriters.org.
Website: www.jamesriverwriters.org
Marty Guise, Executive Director, Lay Renewal Ministries, St. Louis, MO. Phone (314) 647-0717. E-mail: mguise@layrenewal.com.
Website: www.layrenewal.com

VIRTUAL MEETINGS AND DISTANCE SOLUTIONS

Webinar Presentations Involve Members, Generate Revenue

Bite-sized nuggets of professional development — that's how Debren Ferris, program manager at the International Society for Technology in Education (ISTE),Washington, D.C., describes the growing phenomenon of webinars.

Debren and her staff have become experts in the field over the past three years, producing three-dozen one-hour webinars each academic year.

Using Adobe Acrobat Connect Pro — a Flash-based software application available from Adobe Systems Inc. (San Jose, CA) that requires no download or installation on the part of users — as a platform, the presentations they develop offer a variety of lessons to ISTE members.

While a webinar may be a fundamentally individual form of education, Debren and her staff strive to make the webinars as interactive as possible. In the primary series, participants hear the audio presentation over Voice Over Internet Protocol (through their computer speakers), follow slides and video on their screen, and use a chat pod to message one another and type questions to the presenter. In a smaller but more interactive series, participants are introduced to an online tool, given the chance to use and experiment with it, then helped to upload their results and discuss the experience.

 ISTE webinars typically draw 60 to 80 participants, while well-attended sessions can attract 160 attendees, and free-to-the-public sessions (ISTE offers two each year) can top 400 attendees.

Though serving only a fraction of ISTE's total membership, the webinar program is an important revenue-generating venture, says Ferris. Individual webinars cost $50 for members and $125 for nonmembers. Members and non-members can also buy yearly all-access passes for $795 and $1,975, respectively. Archived webinars are available for $20 as well.

In addition to professional development, the program provides a valuable source of outreach to potential members.

Find Top-notch Webinar Presenters

Wondering where to find webinar presenters?

Debren Ferris, program manager at the International Society for Technology in Education (ISTE), Washington, D.C., has simple advice: research, research, research.

"Conference and workshop listings are a great place to start," she says. "Reading publications, Googling possible leads, contacting authors of articles you find interesting — it's a lot of research, but it's a reliable way to find what you need."

This year, Ferris says, they are experimenting with sending a request for webinar proposals. This approach, she says, will help identify presenters more familiar with the realities of a webinar presentation — a format that can intimidate even the most seasoned speakers.

Though only seven percent of webinar participants are non-members, Ferris says it is common for such contacts to join ISTE.

For organizations looking to start their own webinar program, Ferris says the topic of presentation can make all the difference. "Talking-head type lectures don't go over very well," she says. "Presentations based primarily around theory and concepts also are not ideal. People want things they can put into use tomorrow. Free and low-cost tools are very popular. People will always take tools over pedagogy."

She also suggests mindfulness about the program's pricing structure, avoiding both free webinars, which suggest a lack of value, and over-priced presentations that attract few participants. "You really need to be in touch with what your audience can afford and is willing to spend," she says.

Source: Debren Ferris, Program Manager, International Society for Technology in Education, Washington, D.C. Phone (800) 336-5191. E-mail: Dferris@iste.org

Social Media and Communications Technology: Essential Strategies for Nonprofits and Associations.
Edited by Scott C. Stevenson.
© 2011 Stevenson, Inc. Published 2011 by Stevenson, Inc.

Social Media and Communications Technology

ENHANCING E-NEWSLETTERS

The relationship between e-newsletters and traditional newsletters illustrates an inescapable conundrum of our rapidly-evolving media landscape: some things are the same between old and new, some things are different, and it's often difficult to tell which is which. Successfully navigating these challenges will allow your organization to connect with its supporters and stakeholders in the ways that are the best for them — and for you.

What's Your Lead E-Story?

While many large organizations outsource the creation and publication of their e-newsletter, that takes money. If you don't have the budget for that, don't worry. You can still create an e-newsletter that your subscribers will want to read. You just need to know what story issue you wish to make your lead.

Mike Counter, director of media relations at St. Norbert College (De Pere, WI) and his team publish a monthly e-newsletter that is delivered to roughly 10,000 alumni, parents and friends of the college. He says his team puts their e-newsletter together as if it were a local newscast. "We try and have a lead story, which, in our case is usually something academic," says Counter.

The process of coming up with that lead story — the one that will impact or affect subscribers the most — begins a month before the newsletter is published. Counter gathers his news team, a group from the communications department, to hash out what stories should be included in the e-newsletter and assigns writers to those stories.

You may also consider hiring writing talent on a regular or as-needed basis.

At St. Norbert's, Counter says, "We also hire freelance writers in some cases to help with work load or get a different perspective on a story."

Counter also points out that a good e-newsletter will have content people can count on. "We always run Ask the

---

E-Newsletters Aren't Just for Outsiders

While many organizations focus electronic newsletters on customers and volunteers, e-newsletters can be a great way to communicate with smaller or specific groups as well, says Mike Counter, media relations director, St. Norbert College's (De Pere, WI).

To create the college's internal e-newsletter, SNC News, students, faculty and staff submit information using an electronic form on the school's website. The communications department staff proofs and edits submissions. Information that makes the cut is included in the electronic newsletter, which goes out three times a week during the school year and on a limited basis in summer.

Abbot which has become a popular feature readers expect each month." In addition, the e-newsletter will always have at least one article dealing with alumni. And finally, don't forget to cross-promote. Each month's e-newsletter features an area advertising the campus TV program.

Source: Michael P. Counter, Director of Media Relations, St. Norbert College, De Pere, WI. Phone (920) 403-3089. E-mail: mike.counter@snc.edu. Website: www.snc.edu/communications/

Cater E-newsletter Content to Target Audiences

 How do you target various audiences to get your message out?

"One way is through e-newsletters. Calvin College (Grand Rapids, MI) has four — Calvin Wire, which offers breaking news and alumni updates; Calvin-Parents (for parents of students); Calvin-Sports Report (featuring the latest on college athletes); and Calvin-Connection, which has information about on-campus programs and events open to the public. This allows us to send our message directly to our constituents, while reaching very distinct audiences. We determined it would be more widely read if the publications were specific to the audience.

"We are also able to inform and remind neighbors and friends about learning opportunities at or sponsored by Calvin and increase attendance at these events, while allowing us to promote photo galleries and video, too.

"Feedback has been mostly positive. We get a lot of thank-yous and many people stay on the lists long after their child has graduated.

"Our distribution frequency varies from twice a month with Calvin Wire to daily for Calvin-Sports Report, with each publication going out to anywhere from 500 (Calvin-Connection) to 6,527 recipients (Calvin-Parents)."

Source: Lynn Rosendale, Associate Director Communications and Marketing, Calvin College, Grand Rapids, MI. Phone (616) 526-6861. E-mail: lrosenda@calvin.edu

---

ENHANCING E-NEWSLETTERS

Web-based Options Help Stop Communications Budget Drain

Whether to save on production costs, speed up dissemination of information or link to your supporters in the trendiest way possible, look for electronic, web-based options to communicate with your constituency.

Turning to electronic options helped Shelly Grimes rise to a challenge her first day on the job as marketing and public relations coordinator for the Crossroads of America Council of the Boy Scouts of America (Indianapolis, IN), when she learned the organization's leaders felt they were receiving outdated information in their printed newsletters.

That was June 2007. Six months later, the council switched to electronic communications formatting, with the transition project staffed entirely by student volunteers from Indiana University-Purdue University Indianapolis (IUPUI).

The council now produces four versions of its monthly electronic newsletter for various audiences, including volunteers, parents and scouts. Grimes says print is an important component of the overall mix, and the group continues to produce a quarterly print newsletter for recognition and feature stories.

Budget was a secondary — though significant — consideration for transitioning to web-based communications, Grimes says. "Not only was it a more cost-effective option, but it has served our leaders better. We've gotten overwhelmingly positive feedback," with newsletter subscriptions jumping from 4,000 to 7,600 in the 18 months since the launch of the electronic vehicles.

The latest technological tools and toys can boost nonprofits' bottom lines beyond improving communications.

At St. Mary's Food Bank (Phoenix, AZ), for example, a global positioning system (GPS) purchased with grant money is helping organizers plan more efficient truck routes and cut operating expenses. Program leaders project the collection of more goods without the need for additional trucks and employees, plus savings of $50,000 annually in fuel expenditures.

Sources: Shelly Grimes, Marketing and Public Relations Coordinator, Crossroads of America Council/Boy Scouts of America, Indianapolis, IN. Phone 317-925-1900, ext. 224. E-mail: sgrimes@bsamail.org

---

Postcard Replaces Newsletter In Blog-driven Option

Kivi Leroux Miller (Lexington, NC) president of EcoScribe Communications and Nonprofit Marketing Guide.com, advocates a balanced strategy of online communications and creative print tactics.

For example, in response to some nonprofit leaders lamenting they can only afford to send their print newsletters twice a year, Miller suggests creating full-color postcards, which — at one-third the cost of a four-page color newsletter — can go out six times a year for the same expenditure.

So effective is an attractive postcard, says Miller, that organizations may consider dropping newsletters altogether and augmenting the postcards with informative Web content.

Sources: Kivi Leroux Miller, author, Kivi's Nonprofit Communications Blog, Lexington, NC. Phone (336) 499-5816. E-mail: Kivi@ecoscribe.com. Blog: www.nonprofitmarketingguide.com/blog/category/print-newsletters

---

Website Landing Page Keeps Subscribers in Loop

When staff at Bates College (Lewiston, ME) created a new format and distribution system for BatesNews — an online news synopsis with links to more information — they wanted to ensure people followed.

To accomplish this, Bryan McNulty, Bates' director of communications and media relations, says they created a landing page that guides people easily from the old e-newsletter to the new format.

In the last two issues of the old e-newsletter, they ran this message at the top of the page inside a yellow banner:

"BatesNews, the monthly update created for alumni, parents and friends of Bates, is moving to a new format and using a new distribution system. BatesNews was created as and will remain a quick scan for busy people, with links to more information. To continue receiving BatesNews, you will need to opt-in here (clickable web link)."

The opt-in-here link takes visitors to the landing page (http://home.bates.edu/elements/subscribe-batesnews/), where they connect with the college's publications and any of their social media accounts.

McNulty says the landing page not only bumped up the number of subscribers to the monthly digest, but also the daily, weekly and by-topic subscribers as well.

Source: Bryan McNulty, Director of Communications and Media Relations, Bates College, Lewiston, ME. Phone (207) 786-6330. E-mail: bmcnulty@bates.edu

Eight Tips for Writing Engaging Website Copy

Whether launching a new website or redesigning an existing one, keep some key tips in mind when developing the all-important copy that will fill your Web pages.

Joyce Remy, senior editor with the communications firm, IlluminAge (Seattle, WA), offers information that can help nonprofits create website content that both meets the needs of Web users while getting the most value from their website investment:

1. **Consider the other reader — the search engine.** For search engines to find website pages, the pages must include keywords likely to be used by people trying to find your organization. If your organization is a food bank, use terms on your site such as "feeding the hungry" and "food shelf." "As you craft copy, it is important that your keywords sound natural to the readers," says Remy.

2. **Web users are usually seeking a particular piece of information.** Unlike a brochure or ad, websites come with high expectations as an information source, Remy says. "Tailor your language accordingly, offering customers concrete facts, engagingly presented, about all the services your organization offers."

3. **Users navigate your site in a non-linear fashion.** Because Web users can move freely through the site, it is vital that your text doesn't depend on information found on previous pages. Make a good impression on every page, realizing that page users may arrive on a page other than your home page as they navigate the Web.

4. **Persons read Web pages differently than they read other types of copy.** Remy says studies indicate website visitors usually begin with a quick initial once-over when visiting a page. Visual cues such as short paragraphs, bullet points, subheads and white space ensure they can find what they want quickly.

5. **Compared to the printed page, reading on a computer screen is hard work.** As you begin constructing your text, write long and edit to short. Once capturing your basic points, you can usually trim quite a bit and not lose the meaning.

6. **The text of your website doesn't stand alone.** Elements such as logo and contact information, images, navigation buttons and consistent footers allow users to quickly figure out what is available on the site and constantly interact with your text. This can help keep copy concise.

7. **Hyperlinks add a new dimension.** This option allows readers to go to a different spot on the page, different page on your site or to another site entirely. "Hyperlinks give your users the choice of learning about something in greater depth, but don't overdo it," Remy says. "Links can be distracting and once readers leave a page, they may not return."

8. **Use website content area wisely.** "Viewers may not know about your organization. Be clear, concise and thorough when describing the services, geographic areas served and your organization's history, staff or philosophy."

Source: Joyce Remy, Senior Editor, IlluminAge Communication Partners, Seattle, WA. Phone (800) 448-5213.
E-mail: joyce@illuminage.com

Reward Your E-mail Newsletter Readers

If you want people to read your e-newsletter instead of deleting it from their e-mail inbox, you need to make it worth their time. One way to do so is to give them a gift, says Web marketing expert Damian Davila, CEO of Idaconcpts.com (Honolulu, HI), an online marketing and Web analytics site.

"Make good use of the law of reciprocity," Davila says, "and provide something really useful and free to your e-mail recipients."

What kind of rewards can you give? Davila calls the e-mail newsletter from Shutterfly (Redwood City, CA), called Wink, "the king of e-mail newsletters that includes a freebie. They offer readers two free photo strip credits."

And while Shutterfly is a for-profit business, nonprofits can easily follow its lead. Davila recommends offering a product or service that your customers, clients and volunteers would find interesting. "Provide a carrot that is truly valuable and reinforce to your readers how much they can achieve through your gift."

Source: Damian Davila, CEO, Idaconcpts.com. E-mail:damian@idaconcpts.com. Website: http://idaconcpts.com.
Blog: http://idaconcpts.com/category/4-tips-for-a-successful-email-newsletter/

Three Steps to E-Newsletter Success

Web marketing guru Damian Davila, CEO of the online marketing and web analytics site, Idaconcpts.com (Honolulu, HI), shares his top e-newsletter tips:

Make it short and sweet: What is its purpose? "You should be able to answer that question in just one sentence." An e-newsletter doesn't have to be long to be effective as long as it focuses on one main topic.

Spotlight people: "Show how real people make actual use of your services."

Showcase community spirit: Make sure readers understand how your nonprofit helps the community and how they can join you in doing so.

Social Media and Communications Technology

AUGMENTING FUNDRAISING WITH SOCIAL MEDIA

Few areas of nonprofit operation have been as impacted by new communications technologies as fundraising. Social media services have not only changed the process of interacting with donors and prospects, they have created entirely new forums for solicitation. Mastering these new realities might well mean the difference between a year in the red and a year in the black.

Social Networking as a Fundraising Tool: Myths Versus Realities

To innovate the approach to fundraising, St. Olaf College (Northfield, MN) has joined the universe of social networking. St. Olaf can be found on Twitter, Facebook, Myspace and LinkedIn. In addition, St. Olaf reunion volunteers have created class-specific groups and fan pages to promote their reunions.

Matt Fedde, associate director of annual giving, answers questions on what social networking means for higher education fundraising:

Why did you decide to try social networking as a fundraising tool?

"We thought, 'all good online social networking is free, so why not?' The decision to get involved was easy and so was creating the accounts. The tricky part now is trying to figure out how to create quality content for these accounts and to figure out how our presence on these sites can translate into increased gifts to the annual fund."

After gaining friends/fans/contacts, what kind of maintenance does the site require?

"The only social networking service I've been really excited about is Twitter. So it's the one that I've really put energy into in terms of content and reaching out to fans/followers. I look each follower up in our alumni database — if there's a match I send a hello message, welcoming them to give me suggestions for improvements. There is good potential for growth with this — we could do Tweet-ups or target e-mail messages or any number of different targeted messages or events. The nice thing is there's no fee to have an account on any of these sites, and we don't pay someone to create content. Most tweets are auto-generated from official college RSS feeds. Depending on my workload, I may spend zero to three hours a week maintaining the accounts.

"We are considering implementing personal fundraising sites. They were very successful with the Obama campaign, and I've seen them for friends running marathons. But the cost to implement them is fairly high, and there is some uncertainty that the success they have in irregular, deadline-oriented fundraising projects will be able to translate to giving annually to an educational institution."

What kind of response has your office seen to their social networking efforts?

"One challenge has been to quantify the response we've had.

There's no real way to know if our presence on these sites results in increased giving.... Our official annual giving Facebook account has 20 fans. The official St. Olaf Alumni Facebook group has about 2,500 members.... An unofficial, renegade and fairly inactive Facebook St. Olaf College fan page has 3,000 fans. By contrast, our Myspace had 37 views in the past year. Then, our alumni LinkedIn group has 2,250 members. Our Twitter has 500 followers (20 to 30 of whom are traceable alumni) and each tweet link gets four to 35 clicks.

"In terms of Facebook fundraising, an attempt to raise money via Facebook 'cause' bore only $35 in revenue. But when comparing FY '08 to FY '09, we saw a 60 percent increase in the number of online gifts and a 38 percent increase in amount raised through our gift site. Our social networking presence could have contributed to this, but if I were to guess, I'd say that it's more of a national trend than a result of our hard e-work."

> **Check Out**
> **Social Network Sites**
> ✓ LinkedIn (www.linkedin.com/groupInvitation?gid=41543&sharedKey=518C733A86F2)
> ✓ Myspace (www.myspace.com/ucsantabarbara)
> ✓ Twitter (www.twitter.com/macalester)

What are your other fundraising efforts and their relative success? Which are innovative or new for St. Olaf? How are social networking efforts similar/dissimilar to these?

"Within annual giving, our primary programs are volunteer (reunion and non-reunion), direct mail, e-mail, phoning and the Senior Class Campaign.... Our primary work has been to shift focus from institutional fundraising (solicitation that comes from the college: direct mail, e-mail) to peer-to-peer volunteer fundraising (classmate-to-classmate e-mail, phone calls, letters, etc). We've seen great success with this in a handful of classes and are working to replicate their success across all graduated classes. Social networking sites may eventually help with this, but we have yet to figure out exactly how."

Source: Matthew Fedde, Associate Director of Annual Giving, St. Olaf College, Northfield, MN. Phone (800) 733-6523 or (507) 786-3705.

Look to Social Media to Expand Your Fundraising Reach

Social media is one of the trendiest ways nonprofits can raise funds. But with your budget and staff already stretched, how can you implement social media into your efforts?

Take a cue from Big Brothers Big Sisters of America (BBBS), a Philadelphia, PA-based nonprofit that uses many social media venues. Here, Cheyenne Palma, director of development, shares what works for the organization:

Twitter is one of the largest online social networking sites, and it's easy to get lost in all the tweets. How do you use this site productively?

"We try to tweet once a day during the work week and we only follow legitimate people who follow us (trying to avoid the spammers) and we also follow up with a direct message to further engage new followers."

Facebook is another site that is seeing exponential growth. How does your Facebook fan page work for you?

"We have 4,035 fans, an increase of more than 40 percent for the year and our Facebook Causes site (a part of Facebook that allows 501(c)(3) organizations to receive donations through Facebook) currently has 1,896 members who have donated $613. To keep the fan page current and reduce time spent on it, we simply integrated our RSS feed into the site. We've also learned much of our current donor base is active on Facebook and through research and data analysis, we have located nearly 20 percent of them on the site. We've recently formalized our efforts to invite them to connect with us on Facebook."

LinkedIn is known more for its corporate network and as a place for like-minded business people to connect. Do you feel nonprofit fundraising has a place on LinkedIn?

"We are still in the very early stages of determining how we will use LinkedIn. We've begun to identify board members and donors who are active on LinkedIn, but have yet to complete this analysis. We have discussed using the Events module and the Groups functionality to connect with specific donors and supporters on LinkedIn. We anticipate this will

bea much more targeted effort and not as broad an approach as Facebook."

It seems that cell phones can do just about everything now, including depositing paychecks online. Will BBBS dip its toes in the mobile giving waters?

"We are now piloting the ability to donate funds via texting and we have 11 agencies testing text giving. Primarily, we are testing its usage at local events, such as radiothons and baseball games. It appears there is potential where we have a very large, captive audience. Our East Tennessee affiliate received 83 donations in response to a recent radiothon in their market.

"We also anticipate folding mobile giving into our social media fundraising efforts through fundraising widgets. By placing a text-giving widget on select sites, viewers won't even need to go to a separate donation page to contribute; they can simply send a text."

What do you think is important for nonprofits venturing into social media to remember? And if they're not already doing it, should they be?

"It's very important for nonprofits to be involved in social media, particularly because it's the wave of the future. If you look at future generations of donors, it's how they communicate.

"An exaggerated example of this was demonstrated in a news article I read online recently about two teenage girls in Australia trapped in a storm drain — they updated their Facebook status instead of dialing for help! This is the future donor base that fundraisers are looking at tapping into; they need to get on board now, even if it's just to get their name and their message out there.

"Even from a budgetary perspective it makes sense: a few personnel hours per week can lead to donations that you might not otherwise have gotten, and there's no outside overhead to set it up or maintain it if you do it all in-house."

Source: Cheyenne Palma, Director of Development, Big Brothers Big Sisters, Philadelphia, PA. Phone (215) 665-7765, E-mail: cheyenne.palma@bbbs.org

AUGMENTING FUNDRAISING WITH SOCIAL MEDIA

Market Through Social Media

What tips do you have for nonprofits ready to start using social media for marketing and fundraising purposes?

"Remember that social media success is all about content. If you have a compelling message, helpful tips and an engaging mission, you'll find a whole lot of people who want to connect with your organization.... Start slowly, setting up a personal Facebook or Twitter account. Get to know how they work, learn how to connect with others and see how other people and organizations are using these tools. Then think about how your content can support your communication strategies, identify your most appropriate spokespeople and establish your organization's online presence. Plan time to keep your accounts up to date, without overdoing it. People like regular updates, but they'll give up on you if your up-

dates are irrelevant, uninteresting or too frequent."

Mark Miller, Director of Philanthropic Marketing & Communication, Children's National Medical Center (Washington, D.C.)

"Keep your expectations low. Twitter won't solve your organization's issues overnight. Assign someone in your organization to be the point for online contact and let employees know about your social media plans, as they may offer ideas and insight. Make sure you have a plan to engage your audience. Use volunteers to further impact your online presence by engaging in social media on behalf of your organization. Don't be afraid to make mistakes. Just start somewhere to begin building your network. It makes much more sense once you start learning about social media."

— Mark Armstrong, Senior Manager, Internet and New Media, North Texas Food Bank (Dallas, TX)

Book of Blog Entries Creates Memories, Raises Funds

Nick Huber (Alta, IA) started blogging when ALS (amyotrophic lateral sclerosis, also known as Lou Gehrig's disease) forced him to retire from his position as a university sports information director. After his death, a group of friends worked to publish a book of some of his 300 entries and honor his inspirational life.

Sales of "Running With Nick" — a 192-page, soft cover, bound book — raised funds for the ALS Therapy Development Institute (Cambridge, MA).

Project organizer Karna Converse (Storm Lake, IA) shares tips for tackling a similar project with success:

1. Edit minimally. "We edited careless mistakes but didn't automatically change every grammatically incorrect sentence, because we wanted readers to remember Nick's thoughts just as he wrote them. We also wanted to show how technology helped him write for as long as he was physically able — whether he typed words with a keyboard, spoke them into a microphone for translation by voice recognition software or blinked at individual letters via eye gaze software."

2. Decide on the book's format and appearance before setting a price. "We wanted a bound book with heavier-weight paper and a full-color, glossy cover. In other words, it was a project for a printer, not a photocopier — and, based on the number of copies we thought we'd sell, it was a project for a digital printer, not an offset printer. This decision played a major role in setting the book's price."

3. Take pre-orders. "This ensured there were funds to pay the publisher and assured Nick's wife that she wouldn't be left with boxes and boxes of unsold books. We sent press releases to local media but had the most success with a fan page on Facebook, which directed friends to an order form," she says. "We also priced the book to sell ($12) and charged a shipping/handling fee ($2) per order. Some orders cost more than $2 to mail, but because we hand-delivered as many as possible, the shipping and materials cost per pre-paid book was under a dollar."

Source: Karna Converse, Storm Lake, IA. E-mail: conversekj@iw.net

AUGMENTING FUNDRAISING WITH SOCIAL MEDIA

Publicize and Fundraise with Foursquare

Get a jump start on the latest social-media craze by using Foursquare (www.foursquare.com) to drive your fundraising and publicity successes.

On Foursquare, a relatively new social media platform similar to Twitter, users check in by reporting their current whereabouts and post shout outs to let friends know why they like a certain place. In turn, they rely on Foursquare to find nearby friends and get first-person impressions on new places.

How are these functions valuable to a nonprofit organization?

"The value of Foursquare is to strengthen a brand and mobilize supporters," says Jennifer Banks Abreu, founder of Banks Abreu Consulting (Pawcatuck, CT), which specializes in individual-donor development. Abreu says, "While the use of Foursquare for nonprofits is a big topic and there are no set answers since everybody is still experimenting, there are already a couple of really good examples out there that other nonprofits can learn from."

She cites the Brooklyn Museum (Brooklyn, NY) as "a study of how to go all out committing to Foursquare as a social media tool to get support, visits and visibility." The museum's Foursquare page displays profile pictures of everyone who has checked in at the museum recently and spotlights shout-outs they posted. The museum encourages repeat visits by awarding a free membership package to the person who checks in the most at the museum during a calendar month.

Another example is a fundraising drive for Save the Children for its Haiti Relief Fund held in March as part of the South by Southwest Festival (Austin, TX), an annual live-music event. Save the Children collaborated with corporate sponsors Microsoft and Paypal, which agreed to donate 25 cents for every Austin-area check-in during the festival. In just under 48 hours, the organization reached its goal of raising $15,000.

The Save the Children drive, Abreu says, shows how cause marketing — a traditional nonprofit technique — can come alive with the use of social media technology.

Here are Abreu's suggestions for easy ways that a nonprofit organization can make use of Foursquare:

✓ Check in at work. If all your employees and volunteers check in every time they show up for work, that could give you a sizeable Foursquare presence and give your organization some visibility, says Abreu.

✓ Promote events. Anything from holiday donation drives to 5K Fun Runs can be promoted before and during your event using Foursquare, raising awareness, drawing more participants and spectators and, ultimately, donations.

✓ Find local partners. Ask local businesses to donate a preset amount of money to your organization once a set number of users check in at their place of business.

Source: Jennifer Banks Abreu, Founder, Banks Abreu Consulting, Pawcatuck, CT. Phone (860) 599-3440. E-mail: jen@banksabreu.com. Website: http://blog.banksabreu.com

Blog Boosts Fundraising

How can an online conversation help your fund development efforts?

Essentially, a blog is a website and each time you post an update, search engines see that as fresh content and give it a favorable ranking. So if you have a blog for your organization, you are increasing your chances of being found by those who may one day make a gift.

Link your blog to your website and vice versa for even more exposure.

What might you include as blog content that relates to fund development? There's no end to the possibilities. Here are just a few ideas:

✓ Thank those who have funded a recent project and update them on its status. How is it impacting those you serve?

✓ Use your blog to profile those served by your organization. Make a compelling case for why support can and is making a noticeable difference.

✓ Promote upcoming events that the public may want to attend.

✓ Invite your blog readers to vote on ever-changing topics: the next funding project, what they like most about your organization's work and more.

✓ Make a call for volunteers for an event or project.

✓ Make announcements: the kickoff for your annual fund, achieving a milestone, receipt of a major gift, the appointment of new staff, etc.

Check Out Fundraising Blogs For Information, Inspiration

Looking for more information on fundraising and inspiration too? Here are 10 great fundraising blogs:

1. www.donorpowerblog.com by Direct Mail Pro Greg Fox about how to actively involve donors in fundraising.

2. www.fundraisingcoach.com by Marc Pitman, an executive fundraising coach and author of Ask Without Fear.

3. http://hildygottlieb.com by Hildy Gottlieb, president of the Community-Driven Institute and author of "The Pollyanna Principles: Reinventing 'Nonprofit Organizations' to Create the Future of Our World", about boards/governance, fundraising, nonprofit planning, community engagement and more.

4. www.stepbystepfundraising.com by Development Professional Sandra Sims, who shares step-by-step practical resources for fundraisers.

5. www.asmallchange.net by Jason Dick, who works as a campaign manager for a small local Redmond, WA, college, and shares news, information and his views about fundraising for nonprofits.

6. http://beth.typepad.com by Social Media Pro Beth Kanter about how nonprofits can use social media to effect change.

7. http://afprc7.blogspot.com/ by the Association for Fundraising Professionals Resource Center, which shares news and commentary on the fundraising profession and philanthropy.

8. www.theagitator.net by Direct Mail Marketing Pros Tom Belford and Roger Craver, who share fundraising and advocacy strategies, trends and tips.

9. http://majorgiftsguru.com by Tom Wilson, vice president and western regional manager at Campbell & Company and the author of "Winning Gifts: Make Your Donors Feel Like Winners."

10. www.frostonfundraising.wordpress.com by Jay Frost, a 23-year veteran fundraiser, who shares his thoughts on fundraising and philanthropy.

Five Reasons to Think Twice About Mobile Fundraising

The American Red Cross' Text Haiti campaign raised $3 million dollars via $5 mobile phone donations — and interested countless nonprofits in the quickly growing world of mobile fundraising.

Unfortunately the success of such high-profile campaigns can be very difficult to replicate, says Robert Weiner, president of Robert L. Weiner Consulting (San Francisco, CA). Weiner shares five factors he says nonprofits should carefully consider before undertaking a mobile fundraising campaign:

- **Donation size.** Most mobile carriers currently support only $5 or $10 donations. Though this will likely grow in the coming years, it significantly constrains mobile fundraising campaigns, says Weiner.

- **Cannibalization.** A more serious problem of limited donation size is downgraded giving. "If you have donors who regularly donate $100, is it a good idea to ask them for $5, given that some might see answering that appeal as their gift for the year?" asks Weiner. "Cannibalization is one of the biggest risks of mobile fundraising."

- **Cost.** High entry and ongoing costs are another disadvantage. Weiner says setting up a mobile donation system can cost up to $500, with additional monthly fees ranging from $99 to $250 (and up to $1,500 in some cases). A transaction fee — sometimes a percentage, sometimes a fixed amount — is also applied to every text.

- **Delay.** Due to the mechanics of mobile phone transactions, most organizations will wait three months before seeing revenue from a mobile campaign. This delay can be crippling if an organization has a truly urgent need, says Weiner.

- **Donor anonymity.** Because mobile donations yield only a phone number, nonprofits face challenges in stewarding new donors. "You can check the number against your database or hire a marketing service to search for the number, but those are labor intensive and/or expensive," says Weiner. "You can also send a follow-up message with a link to a contact page or a request for an e-mail address, but that requires further steps the donor might not be willing to make."

Despite the drawbacks, Weiner says, mobile fundraising can be an important resource in the professional fundraiser's tool kit: "Young people are very text-responsive and texting might be the best or only way to reach them. The key is employing a diversity of approaches."

Source: Robert Weiner, President, Robert L. Weiner Consulting, San Francisco, CA. Phone (415) 643-8955. E-mail: robert@rlweiner.com

Social Media and Communications Technology

ONLINE MEMBERSHIP SERVICES

What unique and valuable services can you deliver to your members' computers? This has been one of the more perplexing challenges facing member-based organizations. Yet it is also one of their more promising opportunities, for online benefits are far less expensive to administer, can reach members anywhere in the world, and they can be scaled almost without limit, providing a solid foundation for explosive growth.

Draw Attention, Numbers With Socially Networked Membership

Looking for a new way to reach potential members? Consider a socially networked membership that allows members to use free online resources to stay updated on your organization's happenings.

Brooklyn Museum (Brooklyn, NY) recently launched a socially networked membership category entitled "1stfans."

"The idea for 1stfans came out of several conversations Shelley Bernstein, our chief of technology, and I had about community, membership and technology," says William D. Cary, membership manager. "We wanted to create a way for membership to become more accessible for two groups within the museum's community: our Target First Saturday visitors, who are used to visiting the museum at this monthly free event, and our online followers, meaning people who enjoy and participate in the content provided online. Those two groups both demonstrated a strong fondness for the museum, and yet were not taking the next logical step to become members."

They launched the 1stfans membership category during the museum's Target First Saturday event Jan. 3, 2009. A featured artist, Swoon, agreed to do a live printing event for all persons who became 1stfans members on or before that day. More than 60 people signed up for the 1stfans membership during that event.

They publicized the new membership category before the launch event through a museum blog and a press release, as well as through applicable groups on the social networking site, Facebook (www.facebook.com), such as street art, Brooklyn and museum interest groups.

At First Saturday events, staff members wear T-shirts that read "Join 1stfans" and include a number to text from a cell phone to learn more about the membership category.

Cost of a 1stfans membership is $20 a year. Members are invited to the museum's First Saturday events and receive updates via Facebook, Flickr and e-newsletter, depending on their preferences. In addition, they are the only membership category that has access to the museum's relatively new art feed on Twitter.

This membership category is also paperless. One of the advantages of making 1stfans paperless is that it saves the museum money on printing and mailing materials, including membership cards, to the members in this category.

The 1stfans membership is maintained by Bernstein and Cary, who spend considerable time each week, including nights and weekends, updating the 1stfans accounts on Facebook, Twitter and Flickr.

As of March 2009, the new category had 312 members spread across four continents, says Cary, adding: "We've been very encouraged by the response so far, and we're happy to have 1stfans grow organically, so we can get to know everyone personally as they join."

Source: William D. Cary, Membership Manager, Brooklyn Museum, Brooklyn, NY. Phone (718) 501-6436.
E-mail: William.Cary@brooklynmuseum.org

Grow Your Online Benefits

To expand your membership, consider offering online membership and/or benefits.

Online membership is central to the Metropolitan Museum of Art (New York, NY) says Nina Diefenbach, vice president for development and membership. Its Met Net membership category boasts more than 30,000 members (almost a quarter of all members) and is the Met's fastest growing membership level.

Along with unlimited museum admission, Met Net offers access to a members-only website section, audio tours highlighting portions of the museum's collection, exclusive interviews with Met curators and researchers, and screen savers with images from its permanent collection.

Online benefits being developed include converting articles written by museum curators to downloadable PDF files, growing the museum's collection of informational podcasts and allowing members to make reservations for the Trustee Dining Room on the museum website.

Not only can online services benefit numerous members simultaneously, they need not be labor intensive, says Diefenbach. She notes that several of the Met's online benefits were simply adapted or repurposed from other initiatives under way.

Source: Nina Diefenbach, Vice President for Development and Membership, The Metropolitan Museum of Art, New York, NY. Phone (212) 570-3753. E-mail: Nina.diefenbach@metmuseum.org

Reduce Costs, Draw Members With Electronic Memberships

Looking to offer lower-maintenance membership options while at the same time reducing expenses? Offer an online-based electronic membership, or e-membership.

- **The basic idea.** Most e-memberships offer a savings of $10 to $25 and hinge on replacing a hardcopy newsletter or journal with an electronic equivalent. The plan of the National Council of Teachers of Mathematics (Reston, VA) is typical, reducing fees for e-members by $12 and substituting online subscriptions for print journals.

- **International E-membership.** Many associations focus e-membership on international members to avoid the high cost, delivery delays and special handling requirements of sending mail overseas. The National Science Teachers Association (Arlington, VA) is one example, restricting eligibility for e-membership to those residing outside the United States and U.S. territories.

- **E-membership as a type, not a category of membership.** Many organizations offer e-membership as a stand-alone category of membership. The National Flute Association, (Santa Clarita, CA) however, offers it as a type of membership that can be applied to other categories. Members designate active, student or commercial memberships as either regular or electronic, and dues are then calculated accordingly.

- **Place-based e-membership.** E-membership need not be limited to national or international organizations. The Hunter Museum (Chattanooga, TN) provides an e-membership plan that, in addition to providing unlimited admission for one year, offers "electronic invitations to members-only previews, electronic updates on all Museum events and exhibitions and an electronic version of . . . Hunter's quarterly magazine."

- **No-frills membership.** In many cases e-memberships are almost identical to individual memberships, not always, though. The $20 e-membership offered by the Dixon Gallery and Gardens (Memphis, TN) is a significant savings over its $45 individual-level counterpart, but it grants none of the latter's invitations to exhibition openings or reciprocal access privileges.

Sources: The National Council of Teachers of Mathematics, Reston, VA. Website: www.nctm.org/membership/content.aspx?id=7612
The National Science Teachers Association, Arlington, VA. Website: www.nsta.org/portals/international/emembership.aspx
The National Flute Association, Santa Clarita, CA. Website: www.nfaonline.org/membership/levels
The Hunter Museum, Chattanooga, TN. Website: www.huntermuseum.org/jion/membership/membership-levels
The Dixon Gallery and Gardens,Memphis, TN. Website: www.dixon.org/index. php?Itemid=60&id=38&option=com_content&task=view

Virtual Membership Creates Boundless Opportunities

The Museum of Flight (Seattle, WA) is broadening its scope of membership by introducing a virtual membership option.

The museum currently offers visitors a large on-site campus of restored airplanes spanning from the inception of the airplane to today's models. With the new virtual membership option, the museum's current 20,000 members and new members will be allowed to view cockpits of World War I and II planes including P-41s, as well as Blackbird Spy planes, Concordes and the first jet, Airforce One, online, 24 hours a day.

Virtual members will get a birds-eye view of the cockpits by way of 360-degree high-definition tours, zooming in close enough to read the cockpit dials.

Also included with virtual membership is the ask-a-docent forum where members can submit a question for a response from a knowledgeable docent. This makes for an excellent educational opportunity for airplane enthusiasts and educational institutions.

As a way of introducing the new offering to members and to facilitate interest, Flight Leader, Barnstormer and Barnstormer Gold members have been offered the new virtual membership at no additional cost.

Source: Mike Bush, Director of Marketing, Museum of Flight, Seattle, WA. Phone (206) 764-5720.
E-mail: mbush@museumofflight.org.
Website: www.museumofflight.org

Social Media and Communications Technology: Essential Strategies for Nonprofits and Associations.
Edited by Scott C. Stevenson.
© 2011 Stevenson, Inc. Published 2011 by Stevenson, Inc.

Social Media and Communications Technology

SPECIALIZED AND CUSTOM-BUILT SERVICES

The benefits of Twitter and Facebook are well-known, but sometimes more specialized tools are needed. Whether you are seeking to connect with members, patrons, donors or the public at large, building your own communication system — tailored to the specific needs and circumstances of your organization — can sometimes be just what the doctor ordered.

Web Tool Connects Patients and Families in Real Time

How would you like to have 15,000 visits to just one page of your website annually for five years, with that same page keeping people connected to your organization long after the official relationship ends?

That is what the Mercy Messenger service online tool (https://www.mercycare.org/patients/messenger.aspx) has done for Mercy Medical Center (Cedar Rapids, IA), says Melissa Erbes, marketing specialist. The tool, custom created for Mercy, keeps patients' friends and families updated on the status of a hospitalized loved one. It has also put Mercy on the national scene, serving as a model for other hospitals across the country.

Here's how it works:

1. Patients set up a custom account complete with name, admission date, room number, phone number and other pertinent information — including whether the patient is accepting calls and visits. Patients can also choose to have a friend or family member manage the account on their behalf. The setup process takes minutes.

2. Next, the individual who set up the account can create a customizable e-mail list to keep everyone up-to-date.

Friends and family can sign up to receive immediate e-mail alerts each time a new health status posting has been made, or can log in to review the updates at any time. Patients or patient representatives can add new information to the entire list at any time, including health updates and messages. Family members and friends can also send personal get-well greetings.

3. Patients receive a custom patient ID code, allowing them to determine who can access or receive the information.

There is no cost to anyone to use the service. Mercy even has laptops available for their patients and their families to use for free.

Erbes says the response to the online service has been overwhelming and far-reaching. Patients can even continue to use the tool once they are out of the hospital to keep family updated on their health, providing patients with a no-cost, valuable service and providing Mercy with an opportunity to stay top of mind to their constituents.

Source: Melissa Erbes, Marketing Specialist, Mercy Medical Center, Cedar Rapids, IA. Phone (319) 398-6011.
E-mail: merbes@mercycare.org

Share Message in Virtual World

For a creative way to connect with donors, volunteers and others, create an online world related to your cause.

Members of the Colorado Association of Libraries (CAL), Lakewood, CO, can join an interest group based on the virtual world of Second Life from Linden Lab (San Francisco, CA), an online 3D interactive virtual reality program that allows users to socialize and participate in individual and group activities.

CAL has paid for the land rental and custom building design in the virtual online world, offering free participation to all members. Second Life hosts continuing education classes on how to develop personal avatars and has already

hosted several meetings and programs in-world.

The organization is also establishing a presence on Second Life through a virtual library, virtual workshops, conferences and links to websites where members learn more about smart environmental choices.

"The library is not necessarily a place anymore, but an access to information, especially in remote areas," says Jody Howard, association president. "Second Life helps connect members with common interests. It's just another way to use relevant technology to bring people together."

Source: Jody K. Howard, President, Colorado Association of Libraries, Thornton, CO. Phone (303) 859-1242. E-mail: jodyhoward@comcast.net

SPECIALIZED AND CUSTOM-BUILT SERVICES

Networking Opportunities Keep Members Coming Back

To maximize the success of events, Nicole Wilkins, communications manager, Greater Fort Wayne Chamber of Commerce (Fort Wayne, IN) says, the chamber uses two critical tools to keep things running smoothly:

1. **Constant Contact** (www.constantcontact.com) — This e-mail system allows chamber staff to send e-blasts to all members about upcoming chamber offerings, and also offers e-mail marketing and online survey features that are useful for disseminating and obtaining information from members.

2. **WebLink** (www.weblinkinternational.com) — This database management software allows members to RSVP and pay for events on the chamber's website and offers tools for running reports useful for event management.

Source: Nicole Wilkins, Communications Manager, The Greater Fort Wayne Chamber of Commerce, Fort Wayne, IN. Phone (260) 424-1435. E-mail: nwilkins@fwchamber.org

Internal Social Networking Tool Attracts 2,800 Participants

Western Illinois University (Macomb, IL) launched RockeNetwork in May 2006 to help alumni reconnect with former friends, classmates and their alma mater.

The online social network, which now has almost 2,800 alumni participants, is similar to social networking sites like Facebook (www.facebook.com), says Amanda J. Shoemaker, associate alumni director. RockeNetwork lets users add friends to their network, create and join groups (such as geographic location, business groups and campus organizations), blog and send e-mail.

The network is especially helpful for job-seeking alumni, Shoemaker says. "They can use the Careers tab of RockeNetwork to job search, as well as post jobs that they might have open."

RockeNetwork is used as a friendraiser, she says. For example, different geographic groups have been created on RockeNetwork and a number of alumni have used those forums to discuss who is attending alumni/friends events.

The online network "allows alumni to rekindle that great feeling they had when they were students on campus," says Shoemaker. "Perhaps their sorority has a group on RockeNetwork, or the campus organization that they were involved in has a group on RockeNetwork. Reconnecting online with the group and the people who share the same bond gets alumni excited about their alma mater."

She notes that while the online network has many features of familiar social networks, it does not have applications or a wall feature where friends can post messages.

The WIU Alumni Association promotes the program via website (www.rockenetwork.wiu.edu), articles in the alumni quarterly newsletter in its monthly electronic newsletter and in e-mails to alumni reminding them to register and telling them about new features.

"We also share handouts about the network at alumni and friends events and with soon-to-be graduates, and we talk about it as much as we can," says Amy Spelman, alumni director. "WIU President Al Goldfarb mentions RockeNetwork in his commencement speech. We are lucky in that a number of departments/colleges on campus have utilized the program to reconnect with alumni, so they are promoting it as well."

Sources: Amanda J. Shoemaker, Associate Alumni Director; Amy E. Spelman, Alumni Director; Western Illinois University, Macomb, IL. Phone (309) 298-1914. E-mail: ajshoemaker@wiu.edu

---

Tips to Start Internal Social Network

Amanda J. Shoemaker, associate alumni director, Western Illinois University (Macomb, IL), shares her advice for starting an internal social network:

- **Do your research.** "There are a number of networks available now so it is a good idea to find the one that fits your program the best," she says.

- **Get a core group of people to pre-populate the site before it goes live.** These networks only grow when people use them, she says. If users are not active, your network will not be active.

- **Get buy-in from other areas within your organization.** "A number of Western's departments/colleges have created groups on RockeNetwork, so they are working to market it," she says.

- **Promote, promote, promote.** "We post blogs via RockeNetwork to keep alumni updated on campus happenings," to keep the site fresh, she says.

- **Consider building the network internally.** Check with your information technology department to see if they can build it for you. You may have to pay them to build and maintain it, but in the long run, it will probably be cheaper than outsourcing, she says. "However, because we work with a company to provide the service, there are some aspects that we benefit from by working with a company who provides a product to other schools. For example, the careers feature is secure from the user's end, but if a company posts a job, perhaps because they are looking for an employee from Stanford or another such school, our alumni still have access to that job posting."

SPECIALIZED AND CUSTOM-BUILT SERVICES

Hospital Website Connects Patients and Loved Ones

Look for unusual, unexpected and potentially newsworthy ways to serve your constituents.

For more than five years, Presbyterian Hospital (Albuquerque, NM) has offered patients' families and friends the service of its free online greeting card company.

Whether seeking to send congratulations on a new baby, words of support or a get-well wish, persons simply visit the hospital's website, www.phs.org.

As mainstreet supervisor, Toni Gutierrez checks the e-mail in-box twice a day, Monday through Friday; prints the e-greeting cards; and hand-delivers them to patients. Gutierrez says they deliver around 1,100 e-greetings annually, including messages from as far away as Holland and Switzerland.

"This service truly makes our patients happy as they hear from someone who is thinking of them while they are sick, or if they are being congratulated for introducing a new baby into the world," says Gutierrez.

She notes that the messages remain private unless patients request they be read to them.

Source: Toni Gutierrez, Mainstreet Supervisor, Presbyterian Hospital, Albuquerque, NM. Phone (505) 841-1144. E-mail: tgutierre2@phs.org

Should RSS Feeds Be in Your Organization's Future?

If your website changes often or you have breaking news that you disseminate on a regular basis, consider adding RSS feeds.

RSS (Rich Site Summary) is a format for delivering frequently changing website content, and RSS feeds are a simple way of syndicating your content to people who want to receive it. To participate and be able to view your feeds, subscribers download a news reader or aggregator.

With an RSS feed, you provide a free, value-added service to those who are really interested in what you're doing. The feed allows visitors to stay informed by gathering updated content from sites they are interested in, including yours, and you get a more targeted message out to them.

RSS Information, Please

Many online resources offer how-tos, pros and cons of RSS feeds. Here are a few websites to help you learn if RSS feeds are right for your organization:

- www.whatisrss.com
- www.llrx.com/features/rss.htm
- www.microsoft.com/atwork/manageinfo/rss.mspx

Planning Ahead Helps Spell Success for RSS Feeds

Beth Simpkins, media relations coordinator, Johns Hopkins Medicine (Baltimore, MD), says her department learned the hard way about the importance of thinking through all elements of an RSS feed before — rather than after — creating one.

They created a very basic RSS feed, Simpkins says, "and by the time we realized it was taking off, it was too late to change the URL."

She says she wishes she would have put monitoring mechanisms in place, such as those that track the number of subscribers, who is subscribing using what browsers and where subscribers are located geographically.

A potential downside of RSS feeds is that they may limit your ability to capture visitors' information and reach out to them in other ways, as subscribers may bypass signing up for your e-newsletter or limit their visits to your website.

Knowing these challenges can help you when you begin the planning process. Simpkins advises clearly defining how you see the RSS feeds helping your organization; considering a multi-phase plan for implementing the feed system and evaluating what would be involved in changing the system if there was a need.

Source: Beth Simpkins, Media Relations Coordinator, Johns Hopkins Medicine, Baltimore, MD. Phone (410) 955-4288. E-mail: bsimpkins@jhmi.edu

Social Media and Communications Technology

CASE STUDIES: IDEAS WORTH CONSIDERING

Looking to the example of others is a great way to sidestep avoidable mistakes and adopt successful approaches. The following case studies give an overview of the diversity of ways social media is being used by nonprofits across the country.

Social Media Offers New Twist on Old Campaign

Local health insurance company CDPHP has been a supporter of the Regional Food Bank of Northeastern New York (Latham, NY) for a long time. In fact, they have been doing their CDPHP Holiday Appeal to benefit the food bank for the past nine years, in which they donated $5,000, and then pledged to match donations of $100 or more from other companies up to an additional $5,000.

This year, in honor of the 10th anniversary of the appeal, and in recognition of the increasing importance of social media in promotions and fundraising, the partners decided to add a new twist. CDPHP is still offering to match donations of $100 or more up to $5,000, and is also offering to donate $5 for every new "like" on the Regional Food Bank's Facebook account up to an additional $5,000. And the switch seems to be having an impact. So far, $5,000 has been raised in addition to the $10,000 donation from CDPHP. Food Bank Executive Director Mark Quandt says

their number of Facebook friends is growing fairly quickly too, largely due to the CDPHP Appeal.

The campaign has been widely promoted through local media coverage, area newspaper ads, billboard exposure, mail solicitations of CDPHP's vendors and prior food bank donors and an e-newsletter sent to 2,500 food bank supporters.

Quandt says they hope to raise $20,000 through the appeal this year, which seems likely, given the fact that they will continue receiving donations for at least another month. All of the funds raised will be used for the food bank's BackPack Program, which provides nutritious and easy-to-prepare food to disadvantaged children at times when other resources are not available.

Source: Mark Quandt, Executive Director, Regional Food Bank of Northeastern New York, Latham, NY. Phone (518) 786-3691. E-mail: markq@regionalfoodbank.net.

Blogs Bring Student Voices to the Recruitment Process

Imagine being able to follow the lives of several students for a whole year, for an up-close and personal look at what a college is really like, before deciding whether you want to go there.

That's what staff at Bucknell University (Lewisburg, PA) created with A Year in the Life blogs (http://yearinthe-life.blogs.bucknell.edu).

Molly O'Brien-Foelsch, senior writer, says the concept started in 2004. Initial versions chronicled lives of first-year students who posted written entries and photos in eight themed issues a year.

Today, A Year in the Life has been converted into a standard blog. The themes have been eliminated and students blog on topics of their choosing.

University staff, faculty members and student interns recommend students whom they think would be great bloggers. Those candidates then complete an application and selection process.

Bloggers are expected to post at least once a week. They are provided with a list of topics from which to choose, if they wish, but are encouraged to write about anything on their minds as long as the material is appropriate and relevant

to Bucknell's prospective student audience.

Blogger posts are pending until approved by O'Brien-Foelsch, who reviews them with as light a touch as possible.

"The bloggers are great admissions recruiters," she says. "They know their audience, and their enthusiasm for Bucknell is clear."

Bloggers get to highlight their writing and photography abilities, while demonstrating to prospective employers or graduate schools that they are well-rounded, highly engaged and community-oriented.

How does Bucknell benefit from the student blogs?

"The blogs help prospective students get a feel for the culture of the place, the personalities of the students and the possibilities available to them," says O'Brien-Foelsch. "The project is intended to reach the kind of prospective students Bucknell wants to recruit — those who are passionate about academics and want to have personal connections with their professors."

Source: Molly O'Brien-Foelsch, Senior Writer, Bucknell University, Lewisburg, PA. Phone (570) 577-3260. E-mail: mobrien@bucknell.edu

CASE STUDIES: IDEAS WORTH CONSIDERING

Twitter-driven Fundraiser Brings in $10,000 in 10 Days

Nonprofit organizations across the country have had varying degrees of success in harnessing the power of Twitter networking to bring in much-needed donations. Through these groups' trial and error, a best-practices approach is emerging that can help you decide whether a Twitter-based fundraiser will work for you.

One successful group has been the ChristmasFuture Foundation (Calgary, Alberta, Canada), a Canadian-based nonprofit that funds projects worldwide to help erase extreme poverty. ChristmasFuture raised more than $10,000 in the 10 days before Christmas 2008 with its TweetmasFuture fundraiser, says operations manager Leif Baradoy. In all, it brought in about 7 percent of the group's annual budget.

"We've only really been around for two years as an organization, but the key to our success was that we have been able to powerfully represent ourselves through our projects," which include everything from youth arts and leadership programs in Nicaragua to funding a water sanitation project in Sierra Leone, Baradoy says.

The TweetmasFuture campaign didn't have a lot of planning involved, Baradoy says, but it did require a way to donate money online. They sent direct messages on Twitter to many of their 400-plus followers, asking them to donate and/or send out tweets (brief messages sent to subscribers through Twitter) about the campaign. All they had to do then was keep the word going.

Here are Baradoy's tips for a successful Twitter fundraiser:

✓ **Invest in your followers.** Those who have successfully raised thousands of dollars from Twitter activity all have something in common, Baradoy says — they have established a following on the social networking site for at least a year, and regularly send out useful updates (like articles, blog posts etc., that relate to the organization's core mission) to engage their supporters in conversation. In other words, if you build trust with your social network, you build potential for a larger donation pool. "People will only share links and donate if they are convinced it is a good cause," he says.

✓ **Keep it short.** Any longer than 10 days is too long, Baradoy says. You don't want your campaign to become noise in the background.

✓ **Give persons clear direction.** In your initial message, state exactly what you would like them to do, which is basically to donate and retweet, Baradoy says. Don't try to say too much, as tweets are limited to 140 characters.

✓ **Create a fundraiser Web page.** The fundraiser should have its own Web page, and the link to that page should be included in every message you send for the event, Baradoy says. You can shorten the link through the use of computer applications like Tweetdeck, which will also help you keep track of your followers. Include your Twitter feed on that Web page, as well as publicity and links to other important aspects of your group. Make it easy for people to navigate and, of course, to donate.

✓ **Use a hash tag to track the campaign.** Hash tags allow Twitter users to search for all specific content related to that tag, so including one in each message related to the fundraiser is important if you want to see who's supporting you. Baradoy used #TweetmasFuture as a hash tag, but plans to shorten it for future efforts.

✓ **Follow up.** Keep the word going by tweeting about how much money has been raised. Chances are those will be passed on, as well. Publicly thank those who have donated and/or retweeted your messages by sending a reply on Twitter. Consistent involvement in a Twitter campaign is fundamental to success, Baradoy says.

✓ **Don't just take, give back.** ChristmasFuture bought some of its own online donation gift certificates and sent them to the most involved Twitter followers. They could make a donation in their name or pass the gift along to a friend.

Contact: Leif Baradoy, Operations Manager, ChristmasFuture Foundation, Calgary, Alberta, Canada. Phone (866) 629-0516. E-mail: info@christmasfuture.org

Content not available in this edition

CASE STUDIES: IDEAS WORTH CONSIDERING

Use Website Platform for Ongoing Economic Discussion

When staff at Colby College (Waterville, ME) realized that the economic disruption in financial markets was not likely to be short-lived, they also realized the need to communicate the impact the economy was having on the college — sooner rather than later — says David Eaton, director of communications and marketing.

"Even as we worked to fully understand the economic challenges we would face into the future," Eaton says, "it was clear that we needed to communicate, as fully as we could, information about Colby's financial situation with our internal and external constituencies."

Fortunately from the communications standpoint, Eaton says, Colby President William D. Adams had chosen to focus the majority of his semi-annual State of the College address on the college's finances.

"It was really the first time President Adams publicly discussed the effect of the economic disruption on Colby," says Eaton. "And it was clear that many more people — on campus and off — would be interested in hearing what he had to say."

Within a day of the event, communications staff posted a video of the speech, the audience Q&A that followed it and a transcript of the speech on the president's page at www.colby.edu and linked to it from Colby's home page.

From there, the office of communications built "Colby and the Economy," a Web page focused solely on the financial challenges the college faces. The page features State of the College material, additional multimedia content relevant to the topic and frequently asked questions.

Eaton says they add content at appropriate times (e.g., year-end financial update in mid-December; summary of several on-campus forums held following the January board of trustees meeting, etc.).

Eaton says their intention is to continue using the "Colby and the Economy" Web page as one aspect of a multi-faceted effort to keep Colby's constituencies updated on progress in dealing with the financial challenges the college faces.

Check it out at: www.colby.edu/news_events/colby-responds-to-the-global-financial-crisis.cfm

Source: David Eaton, Director of Communications and Marketing, Colby College, Waterville, ME. Phone (207) 859-4356. E-mail: dteaton@colby.edu

Technology Boosts Involvement of Young Alums

One way to do so is to connect with them in a way they understand: online.

Carrie Moore, assistant director, donor relations, Texas Christian University (TCU) of Fort Worth, TX, says keeping young alums involved has been a struggle. But by using viral marketing through websites like Facebook, she says, they are noticing an increase in the number of young alums starting to attend annual events.

Currently, TCU has 2,664 friends on its Facebook alumni site.

In another way that helps young alums stay easily and quickly connected, TCU staff created Froglinks.com, an online community named after the university's mascot, the Horned Frog. This site allows alums to read and leave class notes about their career changes, marriages and growing families; post classified ads; learn about upcoming events; find fellow alums through an online directory; and get career placement help.

Moore says her experience in trying to engage young alums has left her with one bit of advice. "Get involved in all the technology you can, and start now!"

Source: Carrie Moore, Assistant Director, Donor Relations, Texas Christian University, Fort Worth, TX. Phone (817) 257-6965. E-mail: cmoore2@tcu.edu

CASE STUDIES: IDEAS WORTH CONSIDERING

Promotional Campaigns: Break Away From Tradition

If you focus your marketing campaign solely on traditional media, you may be missing out.

Melody Oldfield, director of university marketing, Oregon State University (OSU), Corvallis, OR, says, "You need a fully integrated campaign that combines all communications tactics such as paid advertising, media relations and social media."

OSU's Powered by Orange (PBO) marketing campaign, which Oldfield helped create, has won several awards for its incorporation of social media. PBO is a vehicle to attract various audiences to the university's new contemporary image, she says. "We found that our alumni want to talk about the university and are proud to be a part of the OSU family, but they didn't have a good understanding of who the university is today, and they tended to talk about only sports, a more familiar topic."

So how did OSU's marketing team change the conversation? First, they did their research. They decided their message should focus on Oregon State's positive impact on Oregon's quality of life and how the alumni, faculty, staff and students are making a difference in their communities and environment. From there the PBO campaign was born, a creative effort built on the university's strategic plan that incorporates a website, social networks, videos and a blog.

The backbone of the PBO campaign is a strong website and viral and social media methods to carry messages to the audience. The PBO website is interactive on many levels. First, anyone with an OSU connection is encouraged to provide a testimonial. Second, users can add an orange dot to an online map to demonstrate the nationwide impact of OSU. Finally, visitors can download computer wallpaper, posters and signs to brand their workspace as Powered by Orange.

When it comes to social media, Oldfield says, "The PBO campaign allows both OSU's internal and external audiences to hear from our people about PBO and the university's impact on the community rather than the university always speaking for the people."

One of the PBO's Facebook elements is the Orange Spotlight, which lets people nominate businesses they believe are Powered by Orange. "We use season tickets to (OSU) Beaver football games as an incentive," she says, "and we have received more than 140 nominations."

> ### Promotional Campaign Dos, Don'ts
>
> Creating a multi-platform marketing campaign is a big undertaking. Here are some lessons Melody Oldfield, director of university marketing at Oregon State University (Corvallis, OR), learned while working on its Powered by Orange campaign.
>
> ✓ Do base your campaign in research.
>
> ✓ Do launch and learn in a silent phase. This will allow you to test visuals and use your growing social network as a focus group.
>
> ✓ Don't start a marketing campaign if you do not have resources to keep it going. It takes time to get people engaged and for them to really start internalizing your message. So plan — and budget — for the long haul.

The marketing team then chooses one business each month as its Orange Spotlight. The team does a social media blitz about the business, which is featured on the OSU home page and the PBO website.

The marketing team is also incorporating testimonial videos into the PBO campaign. The videos feature students, faculty and alumni discussing the impact they make on their communities and showing their allegiance to the university by declaring themselves Powered by Orange. Oldfield says they got their first batch of 87 videos by hosting an on-campus event where students were interviewed on camera and given PBO T-shirts. These videos are then posted on the website and social media platforms as well as being featured in traditional paid advertising.

Oldfield says the response to the PBO campaign has been phenomenal, with more than 10,000 members on the campaign's Facebook page.

And while her team has earned several awards for their efforts, she says the alumni and community response has been the best reward. "Our alumni are excited to see OSU be more visible, whether it is through paid advertising, in the news or social media."

Source: Melody Oldfield, Director of University Marketing, Oregon State University, Corvallis, OR. Phone (541) 737-8956. E-mail: melody.oldfield@oregonstate.edu. Website: http://poweredbyorange.com